D0088596

New Poems
by
Robert Browning
and
Elizabeth Barrett Browning
Edited by
Sir Frederic G. Kenyon

Elibron Classics
www.elibron.com

Elibron Classics series.

© 2006 Adamant Media Corporation.

ISBN 0-543-88917-3 (paperback)
ISBN 0-543-88916-5 (hardcover)

This Elibron Classics Replica Edition is an unabridged facsimile
of the edition published in 1914 by Smith, Elder, & Co.,
London.

NEW POEMS

BY

ROBERT AND MRS. BROWNING

Robert Browning
1835
after a daguerrotype from the drawing by an unknown artist

NEW POEMS

BY

ROBERT BROWNING

AND

ELIZABETH BARRETT BROWNING

EDITED BY

SIR FREDERIC G. KENYON

K.C.B., D.Litt.

WITH TWO PORTRAITS

LONDON

SMITH, ELDER, & CO., 15 WATERLOO PLACE

1914

PUBLISHERS' NOTE

₊ IN 1888-9 Robert Browning gave his personal supervision to the issue of his works in an edition of sixteen volumes, to which in 1894 was added a seventeenth volume, being 'Asolando,' the work first published in December 1889, the month in which the poet died.

A complete edition in two volumes appeared in 1896, edited by Mr. Augustine Birrell ; whilst in 1912 was issued the Centenary Edition in ten volumes, under Sir Frederic Kenyon's editorship. To this edition were added ten poems, from various sources, that had not been included before in a collected edition of his works.

At the dispersal of the Browning Collections in May 1913—rendered necessary by the death of the poet's only son, Robert Barrett Browning, which occurred at Asolo on July 8, 1912—twelve new poems by Robert Browning and numerous MSS. by Mrs. Browning were brought to light. Of these, the more important have since been published in the *Cornhill Magazine,* while others, by Mrs. Browning, the MSS. of which had passed into the collection of Mr. Thomas J. Wise, were printed by him, with the sanction of Messrs. Smith, Elder & Co., as owners of the copyright, in a series of little volumes issued in a limited edition of thirty copies each for private circulation.

The present volume is designed to preserve this new material in a permanent form and to enable those who possess editions of Robert Browning's works or of Mrs. Browning's works to complete those editions. To the twelve new poems by Robert Browning have been added ten that are, at present, to be found in the Centenary Edition only; whilst seven more have been included from various other sources, making a total of twenty-nine poems altogether.

Five of the six new poems by Mrs. Browning that are given here are representative of much of her earlier work that remains unpublished; the sixth, ' To Robert Lytton,' is of later date and is a tribute of some importance.

Notes have been prefixed to all the poems collected here giving what is known of their history, both literary and bibliographical.

As regards Mrs. Browning's criticisms, in detail, of her husband's poetry, made before their marriage, the words are appended which Sir Frederic Kenyon wrote with reference to this unique MS. and to the Browning Collections generally in the *Cornhill Magazine* for August 1913.

November 1914

OF THE BROWNING MSS.

THE sale room of Messrs. Sotheby, Wilkinson and Hodge in the first week of May 1913 was a melancholy sight for the lovers of English literature. On the hundred and first anniversary of Robert Browning's birth, a large portion of his library, containing many volumes presented to him and his wife by friends, relations, and admirers, and many with their own autograph inscriptions, were dispersed under the auctioneer's hammer. The next day their personal relics—photographs, busts, chairs, tables, inkstands, blotting books, penwipers, Mrs. Browning's watch, a locket with Milton's hair, and the love token which formed the subject of the Sonnet from the Portuguese beginning ' I never gave a lock of hair away '—passed through the same unsympathetic medium—it may be hoped, into the keeping of those who will cherish them with fitting affection. Two days earlier, a crowded room witnessed the sight of rival dealers competing for the autograph MSS. of 'Aurora Leigh,' of the 'Sonnets from the Portuguese,' and, most intimate and sacred of all, the love-letters of the two poets ; to be informed afterwards that they had been purchased by the victors in the several duels, not on commission for devoted admirers of Robert and Elizabeth Browning, but as articles to be placed in their stock and disposed of to the first purchaser prepared to pay the price to which this competition had forced them up.

It was a sorry sight ; and yet it was not one for which any of those who were concerned in the sale as principals could be blamed. So far as could be ascertained, all the nearest relations on both sides were anxious to avoid a sale, and particularly a public sale, and would have been prepared, if a sale were inevitable, that at any rate the most personal and intimate objects should pass into some national collection, as a permanent memorial of the two poets. But amid the tangle of different interests, the claims of creditors, the advice of lawyers and auctioneers, sentiment had small chance in competition with legal safety, and a public sale could not be averted. With the results, at any rate the creditors will be satisfied, and presumably the lawyers, auctioneers, and dealers will have no cause to complain ; and with this modicum of satisfaction one must be content.

Perhaps one may find other grounds of consolation. The disposal of the minor volumes in the poet's library will, no doubt, have enabled many of the devotees of Robert Browning to secure as mementos books which once belonged to him, and which bear inscriptions in his handwriting. The larger manuscripts were few in number. There was, of course, first of all in sentimental interest, the wonderful collection of those 284 letters which Robert Browning wrote to Elizabeth Barrett between January 10, 1845, and September 19, 1846, and the 287 which he received from her during the same period. These, so far as is at present publicly known, await a purchaser who will make a sufficient advance on the £6550 for which they were knocked down by Messrs. Sotheby. There was the MS. of Robert Browning's last volume, 'Asolando,' purchased for £990—it is understood for America. There were two copies, one perfect and one imperfect, of the 'Sonnets from the Portuguese,' Elizabeth Barrett's high-water mark in poetry, and there was the complete MS. of 'Aurora Leigh,' which Ruskin declared to be the greatest poem in the English language. Further, there were several hundreds of Mrs. Browning's

letters, before and after marriage, to various corre-
spondents, of which the cream has, no doubt, in the
main been skimmed off for previous publication,
but of which many remain unpublished. With
regard to the ' Asolando ' volume, which the poet
intended to go to Balliol College, with the rest of his
MSS. from ' Balaustion ' to the ' Parleyings,' and
which his son retained only for his own lifetime,
one may regret that their expressed desire has been
baulked of its fulfilment ; but with respect to the
others, however much one may wish that they could
have remained in England, it is only fair to remember
that America, where appreciation of both poets, and
especially of Robert Browning, was earlier and more
enthusiastic than in England, has earned the right
to possess any of these relics which she cares to
acquire, and will respect them not less than they
would have been respected here. Readers of Mrs.
Browning's letters will not doubt that both of them
would have gladly recognised the claims of America
in this respect. And it is to be remembered, finally,
that the two greatest MSS. of all, the complete ' Ring
and the Book ' and the copy of the ' Sonnets from
the Portuguese ' which Mrs. Browning gave to her
husband in the early days of their marriage (pushing
them into his pocket and hastily retiring from the

room), which were until recently in the hands to which they were given by the poet and by the poet's son—those of the late Mrs. George Murray Smith, the wife of Browning's publisher and most valued friend—are still treasured in her family. It is also good to know that the surviving copyright in all things Browning now belongs to the firm which have been the Browning publishers since 1868, Smith, Elder & Co.

But among the minor manuscripts were many which have a literary as well as a sentimental interest. One might perhaps wish that the unpublished verses of both poets had been destroyed by them out of hand when once the decision had been taken not to publish them. Such waifs and strays are a permanent difficulty to editors. If the author is sufficiently eminent, publication of everything of his that remains above ground is eventually inevitable, and an editor is torn between the natural desire to make his edition complete, and his equally natural reluctance to print matter which is not worthy of its author, and which the author himself did not consider worthy of publication. The ultimate solution is probably some limbo of an appendix, which can be searched once for all by the curious and then left to its obscurity. Yet even in such an outer darkness one does

not care to meet Browning's freakish rhymes to
'rhinoceros' or 'Timbuctoo'; while it is an in-
justice to two, if not three, of the stars of our Victorian
literature to reprint, at any time or in any place,
the 'Lines to Edward FitzGerald.'

One little group of manuscripts, however, in the
delicate handwriting of Mrs. Browning, has a special
interest, personal and literary, and its publication can
do no harm to anyone. In September and October
1845 Robert Browning was engaged in preparing for
the press the poems which were published in November
as Part VII of his 'Bells and Pomegranates,' under
the general title of 'Dramatic Romances and Lyrics.'
Five of them had previously appeared in *Hood's
Magazine* during 1844 and the spring of 1845, and
these had come to Miss Barrett's notice in July;
the rest were sent to her in manuscript and proof in
the course of the autumn. Her criticisms were asked
for honestly and were sent loyally; and they lie
before us now in these little sheets. They are not
criticisms in the larger sense of the term, not appreci-
ations of the general scheme of the poems, but merely
suggestions for verbal alterations, the little queries
which a friend may make of a friend's work, especially
when the critic is himself (or herself, as in this instance)
a poet. Those who do not care for the minutiæ of

poetic production, or are content with the result
without inquiring as to the means, will have no con-
cern with these; but some of those whose interests
are bound up with the poetry of Robert Browning
may care to see how the poet who was afterwards
to be his wife helped him.

Those who have any acquaintance with the
bibliography of Browning's poetry (and some such
acquaintance is really essential to an understanding
of the development of his genius, since the familiar
classification of the shorter poems has obscured
their chronological order) know that the original
'Dramatic Romances and Lyrics' of 1845 are a
very different group of poems from the 'Dramatic
Romances' as they appear in every edition after 1863.
Part VII of 'Bells and Pomegranates' consisted
of twenty-one poems. Of these, only six remained
under the heading of 'Dramatic Romances' in 1863.
Thirteen were transferred to the 'Dramatic Lyrics,'
and two to 'Men and Women,' where we still find
them to-day. Of the original twenty-one, twelve
receive annotations from Miss Barrett in the papers
now before us, in addition to 'A Soul's Tragedy'
and 'Luria,' which formed the eighth and last part
of 'Bells and Pomegranates,' published a few months
later, in April 1846. These twelve poems include

the five which had previously appeared in *Hood's Magazine* (' The Tomb at St. Praxed's,' ' The Flower's Name,' ' Sibrandus Schafnaburgensis,' ' The Laboratory,' and ' The Boy and the Angel '), together with ' How they brought the Good News,' ' Pictor Ignotus,' ' Italy in England,' ' England in Italy,' ' The Confessional,' ' Saul,' and ' Time's Revenges.' In addition, some comments (but of a more general nature) on ' The Lost Leader,' ' The Lost Mistress,' ' Home Thoughts from Abroad,' ' The Flight of the Duchess,' ' Earth's Immortalities,' ' Nay, but you who do not love her,' ' Night and Morning,' ' Claret and Tokay,' and ' The Glove,' which constitute the rest of the volume, appear in the published letters, and so complete Miss Barrett's criticisms on the whole group of poems.

These criticisms for the most part relate to small details of phrase or rhythm. It is curious to find Elizabeth Barrett, whose ear, to judge from her own poetry, was not remarkably sensitive, criticising the imperfect rhythm of Robert Browning. But Miss Barrett was a better critic than poet at this period (which, be it remembered, was before the ' Sonnets from the Portuguese ' and ' Aurora Leigh ') ; and it is rather in imperfect rhymes than in defective rhythms that her ear is mostly at fault. On the other hand, Browning in his earlier lyrics had a certain staccato jerkiness, of which he subsequently cured himself ; and most readers will agree that his correspondent's criticisms were justified. Miss Barrett's notes upon ' Saul ' will illustrate this point, and at the same time furnish a fair sample of her comments in general:

> ' Nor till from his tent

Would you not rather write " until," here, to break the course of monosyllables, with another reason ?

> ' For in the black mid-tent silence
> Three drear days—

A word seems omitted before " silence "—and the short line is too short to the ear—not to say that " drear days " conspires against " dread ways " found afterwards. And the solemn flow of the six lines should be uninterrupted, I think.

' The entrance of David into the tent is very visible and characteristic,—and you see his youthfulness in the activity of it—and the repetition of the word " foldskirts " has an Hebraic effect.

> ' But soon I descried
> Something more black than the blackness.

Should it not be " A something "—more definitely ? And the rhythm cries aloud for it, it seems to me.

> ' The vast, upright—

Quaere—" *the* upright " . . . for rhythm.

b

> ' Then a sunbeam burst thro' the blind tent-roof
>   Showed Saul.

Now, will you think whether to enforce the admirable effect of your sudden sunbeam, this first line shall not be rendered more rapid by the removal of the clogging epithet " blind "—which you repeat, too, I believe, farther on in the next page ? What if you tried the line thus,

> ' Then a sunbeam that burst through the tent-roof—
>   Showed Saul !

The manifestation in the short line appears to me completer from the rapidity being increased in the long one. I only *ask*. It is simply an impression. I have told you how very fine I do think all this showing of Saul by the sunbeam—and how, the more you come to see him, the finer it is. The " all heavily hangs," as applied to the king-serpent, you quite feel in your muscles.

' The breaking of the band of lilies round the harp is a relief and refreshment in itself after that dreadful sight. And then how beautifully true it is that the song should begin so . . . with the sheep—

> ' As one after one
>   Docile they come to the pen door—

But the rhythm should not interrupt itself where

the sheep come docilely—and is not a word wanted
. . . a syllable rather . . . before that " Docile " ?
Will you consider ?

    ' " The long grasses stifling the water " . . . How
beautiful *that* is !

> ' One after one seeks its lodging
> As star follows star
> Into the blue far above us,
> —So blue and so far !

It appears to me that the two long lines require a
syllable each at the beginning, to keep the procession
of sheep uninterrupted. The ear expects to read every
long and short line, in the sequence of this metre,
as one long line,—and where it cannot do so, a loss
. . . an abruption . . . is felt—and there should
be nothing abrupt in the movement of these pastoral,
starry images—do you think so ? Is it not Goethe
who compares the stars to sheep ? Which you
reverse here.

> ' Would we might help thee, my brother ?

Why not, " Oh, would," &c.—it throws a wail into
the line, and swells the rhythm rightly, I think.

> ' Next she whom we count
> The beauty, the pride of our dwelling—

Why not " For the beauty " or " As the beauty " ?

> ' But I stopped—for here, in the darkness
> Saul groaned.

Very fine—and the preceding images full of beauty and characteristic life !—but in this long line, I just ask if the rhythm would gain by repeating " here " . . . thus . . .

> ' But I stop here—for here in the darkness—

I just ask, being doubtful.

> ' And the shaking of the tent from the shudder of

the king . . . what effect it all has !—and I like the jewels *waking* in his turban !

> ' So the head—but the body stirred not.

If you wrote " So the head—but the body . . . *that* stirred not "—Just see the context.

> ' The water was wont to go warbling
>   Softly and well.

Is not a syllable wanted at the beginning of the short line, to make the water warble softly . . . " right softly " ?

> ' And heard her faint tongue
> Join in, while it could, to the witness—

Would " joining in " be better to the ear ?

> ' And promise and wealth for the future

I think you meant to write " the " before promise.

> ' All I said about the poem in my note, I think

more and more. Full of power and beauty it is—
and the conception, very striking.

' E. B. B.'

That is one little batch of notes, one morning's
work, it may be, of the invalid lying on her back
on her couch, and writing in her tiny hand on tiny
sheets of note-paper—for, as she said, she was a
small woman, and liked to have small things about
her. The reader who will take the pains to compare
the criticisms with the poem as it stands to-day
(remembering that, in its original form, it was printed
in alternate long and short lines, in place of the
uniform long lines to which we are accustomed) will
see that in almost every case Browning had the
wisdom to accept his critic's suggestions. It was
the most useful form of criticism—accepting and
admiring the general conception and treatment,
but suggesting minor improvements in detail which
could be adopted without difficulty. The criticism
which begins by telling a poet to alter his whole
method is rarely of any use.

It would be tedious to go through the other poems
in detail. In the lyric poems Miss Barrett's criticisms
are mostly directed to improvements in rhythm
and the removal of small obscurities. In ' Luria,'

on the other hand, she did good service by discouraging a trick of inversion, and pointing out the greater force given by directness. No one who knows this noble poem will question the inferiority of the first form of these lines (Act I, ll. 139–142)—

> If in the struggle when the soldier's sword
> Before the statist's hand should sink its point,
> And to the calm head yield the violent hand,
> Virtue on virtue still have fallen away . . .

to the simple, directer form in which they now stand. 'Tell me if an air of stiffness is not given by such unnecessary inversions,' says the critic in another instance ; and again, when she has set straight another contorted phrase, 'You allow the reader to see at a glance what otherwise he will seek studiously.' This is a pregnant phrase, which Browning in later years might have done well to bear in mind. Not that the want of directness in some of the later poems, as compared with these of the Italian period, is to be attributed to the loss of his wife's correcting hand ; for we know that the married poets made a point of keeping their work independent and apart until it was ready for the press. Nevertheless, the lesson indicated by these few criticisms seems to have borne fruit in the greater clarity of the poems published between 1845 and 1864 ('Dramatis Personæ'), and was not always forgotten afterwards.

A few more general expressions of opinion may be quoted in conclusion. Of 'Sibrandus Schafnaburgensis,' that delightful story of vengeance on a pedant, Miss Barrett writes :

> Do you know that this poem is a great favourite with me—it is so new, and full of a creeping, crawling, grotesque life. Ah, but . . . do you know, besides, it is almost reproachable in you to hold up John Knox to derision in this way !

Of ' The Tomb at St. Praxed's ' (as the poem was originally called, of which Ruskin said that he knew no other piece of modern English in which there is so much told of the Renaissance spirit) :

> This is a wonderful poem, I think, and classes with those works of yours which show most power . . . most unquestionable genius in the high sense. You force your reader to sympathise positively in his glory in being buried.

She notices also ' the rushing and hurrying life of the descriptions ' in ' England in Italy ' (with its alternative title ' Autumn at Sorrento '), ' tossed in one upon another like the grape bunches in the early part, and not kept under by ever so much breathless effort on the poet's part,' and adds : ' For giving the *sense of Italy*, it is worth a whole library of

travel-books.'   Of the companion poem, 'Italy in
England,' which Mazzini read to his fellow-exiles as a
proof that at least one Englishman sympathised with
them, she says : 'I like the simplicity of the great-
heartedness of it (though perhaps half-Saxon in
character), with the Italian scenery all around—it
is very impressive.'

It is not always easy for the first critic of a new
poem (and Browning's were so new that nothing like
them, except the 'Dramatic Lyrics' in Part III of
the 'Bells and Pomegranates,' had ever appeared in
English literature) to hit on just the features to which
its ultimate reputation is due ; but Miss Barrett does
so again and again with unerring touch.   Of 'Pictor
Ignotus' she says : 'This poem is so fine, so full of
power, as to claim every possible attention to the
working of it : it begins greatly, grandly, and ends
so,—the winding up winds up the soul of it.   The
versification too is noble . . . I cannot tell you how
much it impresses me.'   And she appreciates fully
the verve and vigour of the great ride from Ghent
to Aix :

 You have the very trampling and breathing of the
horses all through—and the sentiment is left in its right
place, through all the physical force and display . . .
I know you must be proud of the poem, and nobody

can forget it who has looked at it once. . . . By the way, how the ' galloping' is a good galloping word ! And how you felt it, and took the effect up and dilated it by repeating it over and over in your first stanza . . . doubling, folding one upon another, the hoof-treads.

The textual criticism of Browning cannot have quite the same value as that of an artist in words, such as Tennyson, the lessons of whose fastidious taste are so well brought out in his son's biography. Nevertheless there is interest in tracing the development of his power of self-expression from the turbid waters of ' Pauline' and the tangled thickets of ' Sordello ' up to the supreme mastery of thought and phrase which marks the fifty ' Men and Women ' of 1855, and which endured through the finest poems of ' Dramatis Personæ ' to the best books of ' The Ring and the Book.' And in the fragments of the story which have here been offered to the sympathetic reader there is the further interest that they form an episode in the beautiful idyll of the love of Elizabeth Barrett and Robert Browning.

FREDERIC G. KENYON.

CONTENTS

PORTRAITS

NEW POEMS

NEW POEMS

THE FIRST-BORN OF EGYPT

[Robert Browning destroyed much of his very early work; this poem and the one that follows it are the only surviving examples. They were written in his fourteenth year, and we are indebted for their preservation to Miss Sarah Flower (afterwards Mrs. Adams, author of ' Nearer, my God, to Thee '), who copied out the two poems in a letter addressed to William Johnson Fox in 1827 (see p. 18). This letter was brought to light at the sale of the Browning Collections in 1913, being purchased with other papers by Mr. Bertram Dobell. Both the writer of the letter and its recipient were friends of the youthful poet. The poems were first printed, in an article by Mr. Bertram Dobell, in the *Cornhill Magazine* for January, 1914.]

THAT night came on in Egypt with a step
So calmly stealing in the gorgeous train
Of sunset glories flooding the pale clouds
With liquid gold, until at length the glow
Sank to its shadowy impulse and soft sleep
Bent o'er the world to curtain it from life—

Vitality was hushed beneath her wing—
Pomp sought his couch of purple—care-worn grief
Flung slumber's mantle o'er him.   At that hour
He in whose brain the burning fever fiend
Held revelry—his hot cheek turn'd awhile
Upon the cooler pillow.   In his cell
The captive wrapped him in his squalid rags,
And sank amid his straw.   Circean sleep !
Bathed in thine opiate dew false hope vacates
Her seat in the sick soul, leaving awhile
Her dreamy fond imaginings—pale fear
His wild misgivings, and the warm life-springs
Flow in their wonted channels—and the train—
The harpy train of care forsakes the heart.

Was it the passing sigh of the night wind
Or some lorn spirit's wail—that moaning cry
That struck the ear ? 'tis hushed—no ! it swells on
On—as the thunder peal when it essays
To wreck the summer sky—that fearful shriek
Still it increases—'tis the dolorous plaint,
The death cry of a nation—

It was a fearful thing—that hour of night.
I have seen many climes, but that dread hour
Hath left its burning impress on my soul
Never to be erased.   Not the loud crash

When the shuddering forest swings to the red bolt
Or march of the fell earthquake when it whelms
A city in its yawning gulf, could quell
That deep voice of despair. Pharaoh arose
Startled from slumber, and in anger sought
The reason of the mighty rushing throng
At that dark hour around the palace gates,
—And then he dashed his golden crown away
And tore his hair in frenzy when he knew
That Egypt's heir was dead—From every home,
The marbled mansion of regality
To the damp dungeon's walls—gay pleasure's seat
And poverty's lone hut, that cry was heard
As guided by the Seraph's vengeful arm
The hand of death held on its withering course,
Blighting the hopes of thousands.—

I sought the street to gaze upon the grief
Of congregated Egypt—there the slave
Stood by him late his master, for that hour
Made vain the world's distinctions—for could wealth
Or power arrest the woe ?—Some were there
As sculptured marble from the quarry late
Of whom the foot first in the floating dance,
The glowing cheek hued with the deep'ning flush
In the night revel—told the young and gay.

No kindly moisture dewed their stony eye,
Or damp'd their ghastly glare—for they felt not.
The chain of torpor bound around the heart
Had stifled it for ever. Tears stole down
The furrow'd channels of those withered cheeks
Whose fount had long been chill'd, but that night's
     term
Had loosed the springs—for 'twas a fearful thing
To see a nation's hope so blasted. One
Press'd his dead child unto his heart—no spot
Of livid plague was nigh—no purple cloud
Of scathing fever—and he struck his brow
To rouse himself from that wild phantasy
Deeming it but a vision of the night.
I marked one old man with his only son
Lifeless within his arms—his withered hand
Wandering o'er the features of his child
Bidding him [wake] from that long dreary sleep,
And lead his old blind father from the crowd
To the green meadows [1]—but he answer'd not ;
And then the terrible truth flash'd on his brain,
And when the throng roll'd on some bade him rise
And cling not so unto the dead one there,
Nor voice nor look made answer—he was gone.

[1] It is to be presumed that these lines were thus italicised by Miss Flower because she wished to draw Mr. Fox's attention to them as being particularly good.

But one thought chain'd the powers of each mind
Amid that night's felt horror—each one owned
In silence the dread majesty—the might
Of Israel's God, whose red hand had avenged
His servants' cause so fearfully.

THE DANCE OF DEATH

And as they footed it around,
They sang their triumphs o'er mankind !
de Stael.

FEVER

Bow to me, bow to me ;
Follow me in my burning breath,
Which brings as the simoom destruction and death.
My spirit lives in the hectic glow
When I bid the life streams tainted flow
In the fervid sun's deep brooding beam
When seething vapours in volumes steam,
And they fall—the young, the gay—as the flower
'Neath the fiery wind's destructive power.
This day I have gotten a noble prize—
There was one who saw the morning rise,
And watch'd fair Cynthia's golden streak
Kiss the misty mountain peak,
But I was there, and my pois'nous flood
Envenom'd the gush of the youth's warm blood.

They hastily bore him to his bed,
But o'er him death his swart pennons spread :
The skilléd leech's art was vain,
Delirium revelled in each vein.
I mark'd each deathly change in him ;
I watch'd his lustrous eye grow dim,
The purple cloud on his deep swol'n brow,
The gathering death sweat's chilly flow,
The dull dense film obscure the eye,
Heard the last quick gasp and saw him die.

PESTILENCE

My spirit has past on the lightning's wing
O'er city and land with its withering ;
In the crowded street, in the flashing hall
My tramp has been heard : they are lonely all.
A nation has swept at my summons away
As mists before the glare of day.
See how proudly reigns my hand
In the black'ning heaps on the surf-beat strand
[Where] [1] the rank grass grows in deserted streets
[Where] the terrified stranger no passer meets
[And all] around the putrid air
[Gleams] lurid and red in Erinnys stare

[1] Paper removed where sealed.

Where silence reigns, where late swell'd the lute,
Thrilling lyre, mellifluous flute.
There if my prowess ye would know
Seek ye—and bow to your rival low.

AGUE

Bow to me, bow to me ;
My influence is in the freezing deeps
Where the icy power of torpor sleeps,
Where the frigid waters flow
My marble chair is more cold below ;
When the Grecian brav'd the Hellespont's flood
How did I curdle his fever'd blood,
And sent his love in tumescent wave
To meet with her lover an early grave.
When Hellas' victor sought the rush
Of the river to lave in its cooling gush,
Did he not feel my iron clutch
When he fainted and sank at my algid touch ?
These are the least of the trophies I claim—
Bow to me then, and own my fame.

MADNESS

Hear ye not the gloomy yelling
Or the tide of anguish swelling,
Hear ye the clank of fetter and chain,
Hear ye the wild cry of grief and pain,

Followed by the shuddering laugh
As when fiends the life blood quaff ?
See ! see that band,
See how their bursting eyeballs gleam,
As the tiger's when crouched in the jungle's lair,
In India's sultry land.
Now they are seized in the rabies fell,
Hark ! 'tis a shriek as from fiends of hell ;
Now there is a plaining moan,
As the flow of the sullen river—
List ! there is a hollow groan.
Doth it not make e'en *you* to shiver—
These are they struck of the barbs of my quiver.
Slaves before my haughty throne,
Bow then, bow to me alone.

CONSUMPTION

'Tis for me, 'tis for me ;
Mine the prize of Death must be ;
My spirit is o'er the young and gay
As on snowy wreaths in the bright noonday
They wear a melting and vermeille flush
E'en while I bid their pulses hush,
Hueing o'er their dying brow
With the spring (?) of health's best roseate glow

When the lover watches the full dark eye
Robed in tints of ianthine dye,
Beaming eloquent as to declare
The passions that deepen the glories there.
The frost in its tide of dazzling whiteness,
As Juno's brow of chrystal brightness,
Such as the Grecian's hand could give
When he bade the sculptured marble ' live,'
The ruby suffusing the Hebe cheek,
The pulses that love and pleasure speak
Can his fond heart claim but another day,
And the loathsome worm on her form shall prey.
She is scathed as the tender flower,
When mildews o'er its chalice lour.
Tell me not of her balmy breath,
Its tide shall be shut in the fold of death ;
Tell me not of her honied lip,
The reptile's fangs shall its fragrance sip.
Then will I say triumphantly
Bow to the deadliest—bow to me !

THE EARLIEST POEMS OF ROBERT
BROWNING

WHEN I was writing my 'Sidelights on Charles
Lamb,' I happened in the course of my search for
materials to look through the volume of *The Monthly
Repository* for 1835. Therein I found, with other
matter on my subject, an article entitled 'An Evening
with Charles Lamb and Coleridge,' over the signature 'S. Y.' I found this so interesting from its
vivid and sympathetic sketches of the two authors
that I searched the volume for other writings with
the same signature. I found that 'S. Y.' was a
frequent contributor of verse and prose to the
magazine. In all these contributions I recognised
the work of a mind 'touched to fine issues,' and I
became very curious as to the personality hidden
behind the mask 'S. Y.' I felt assured the writer
could not be altogether unknown to fame; but I
could find no clue that would connect him—or her—
with any known author. I was particularly struck
with the excellence of the various poems by 'S. Y.,'

and when I printed ' An Evening with Charles Lamb and Coleridge ' in my book, I printed also a poem ' Morning, Noon, and Night ' which I then thought—and still think—worthy of being included in any anthology of English verse.[1]

Some time after the publication of my book I was informed—I cannot now remember by whom—that ' S. Y.' stood for ' Sally,' the usual signature in letters to friends and relatives of Mrs. Sarah Flower Adams, well known as the author of what is now, perhaps, the most popular hymn in our language, ' Nearer, my God, to Thee '; but otherwise, save to a very few, practically unknown. The fame she has hitherto enjoyed, despite its narrow limits, has yet been of a not unenviable kind ; for it would be impossible to name any poem, not of a religious character, which is so often in the minds and on the lips of humanity as the hymn which I have mentioned. It is one which, like Newman's ' Lead, kindly Light,' can never fall into disuse ; since its appeal is universal and does not depend upon any doctrine which may not be subscribed to by the members of any church or creed.

Eliza and Sarah Flower were the daughters of Benjamin Flower, a printer, and a man of liberal

---

[1] It has found its way into at least one anthology.

opinions, at a time when the open avowal of such opinions was extremely likely to lead to unpleasant consequences. He was the publisher of *The Cambridge Intelligencer*, in which paper some of Coleridge's poems first appeared, and to which, when he discontinued his *Watchman*, the poet recommended his readers to subscribe. Some disrespectful remarks, which were printed in the paper, upon Bishop Watson, then famous as the Church's champion against Paine's 'Age of Reason,' were construed as a breach of the privileges of the House of Lords, and the unfortunate publisher was condemned to six months' imprisonment and a fine of a hundred pounds. Yet this seeming misfortune was, it appears, something like a blessing in disguise. Eliza Gould, a Devon schoolmistress, and a reader of *The Intelligencer*, found herself compelled to choose between giving up her school or giving up her newspaper. She was a woman of spirit, and chose rather to sacrifice her school than her liberal opinions. She visited Flower in prison, with the result that a mutual affection sprang up between them ; and this led, on his release, to their marriage. She became in 1803 the mother of Eliza, and in 1805 of Sarah Flower. Like her daughters, she was destined to an early death : she passed away in 1810.

The Flower sisters, it appears, had become acquainted with the Browning family through a mutual friend, a Miss Sturtevant. This happened in 1827, or it may be a year or so earlier. Robert Browning was then between fourteen and fifteen years of age ; and the sisters, naturally enough, took much interest in the ' boy Genius.' He had already written a ' book full ' of verse, which he had entitled ' Incondita,' and which he was ' mad to publish.' His mother showed this book to the sisters ; and Eliza Flower, it is said, admired the book so much that she copied out the whole of it. But perhaps I had better quote from .Mrs. Orr's ' Life of Browning ' her account of this matter :

'The young author gave his work the title of " Incondita," which conveyed a certain idea of depreciation. He was, nevertheless, very anxious to see it in print ; and his father and mother, poetry lovers of the old school, also found in it sufficient merit to justify its publication. No publisher, however, could be found ; and we can easily believe that he soon afterwards destroyed the little manuscript, in some mingled reaction of disappointment and disgust. But his mother, meanwhile, had shown it to an acquaintance of hers, Miss Flower, who herself admired its contents so much as to make a copy of them for the inspection of her friend, the well-known Unitarian minister, Mr. W. J. Fox. The copy was transmitted to Mr. Browning after Fox's death, by his daughter, Mrs. Bridell Fox ;

and this, if no other, was in existence in 1871, when, at his urgent request, that lady also returned to him a fragment of verse contained in a letter from Miss Sarah Flower. Nor was it till much later that a friend, who had earnestly begged for a sight of it, definitely heard of its destruction. The fragment, which doubtless shared the same fate, was, I am told, a direct imitation of Coleridge's " Fire, Famine and Slaughter." '

Mrs. Orr wrote the above from the best information then available; but her statement can now be amplified. It may be true that Eliza Flower copied out the whole of the ' Incondita ' volume for Mr. Fox's inspection; but it is certain that it was not she, but her sister, who first introduced the poems—or at least two of them—to Mr. Fox's notice. We shall see, too, that the letter of Sarah Flower is, fortunately, still in existence, and that it contains, not ' a fragment of verse,' but two complete poems, of quite sufficient length to show of what the young poet was then capable. Nor is the fragment spoken of a direct imitation of Coleridge's ' Fire, Famine and Slaughter.' It may have been suggested by it; but it cannot fairly be called a mere imitation.

EXTRACT FROM A LETTER FROM SARAH FLOWER (AFTER-
WARDS MRS. ADAMS, AUTHOR OF ' NEARER, MY GOD,
TO THEE ') TO WILLIAM JOHNSON FOX.

DALSTON
May 31*st* (1827).

' What in the name of fortune is the girl going to do
with this tremendous sheet of paper ? ' Now dread
the worst my dear Mr. Fox but suspend your judgment
one minute—now in reward you shall hear what a
delicious treat you may expect when you have turned
over a new leaf. Now do not peep. Yes you may just
take one, only one. I do most positively forbid your
reading that Genius's poetry tho' I grant it looks very
tempting until you have waded thro' the prosy part.
No ! No ! I am quite too cunning for that. So now
having done as they do with children (—there—take
your physic there's a good child and then you shall have
something Oh so nice afterwards), shall I tell you whose
mine these gems come from ?—and yet I wish they were
mine with all my soul—and I'm sure it would be worth
all *my* soul if they were—' Bah '—forgive me and if
you knew what a bad muddling cold I have had you
would—They are ' the boy ' Robert Browning's *æt*. 14—
and so they as well as he can speak for themselves.

I do not know of any equally promising work by
one who was no older than Browning at the time these
poems were written ; unless indeed it was that of his
future wife, whose epic of ' The Battle of Marathon '
was a still more juvenile production. Shelley, at
about the same age, was still in his witch, hobgoblin,

and Minerva Press period, and had written nothing but wild and incoherent rhapsodies from which no favourable forecast of his future achievements could possibly have been derived. The feeling we should have for his early writings would be something like contempt, if we did not know that they were the necessary prelude to ' The Cenci ' and ' Prometheus Unbound.' But we can have no such feeling about ' The First-born of Egypt,' or ' The Dance of Death.' Faulty they may be, but there is evidence enough in them that their author had within him the elements from which so many and such vigorous creations were to spring. And those who will take the trouble to search for them will, I am sure, discover in the later work of the poet a good many parallels to lines or passages in these early efforts.

Six months after writing the letter printed above Sarah Flower wrote another, of a very different character, to Mr. Fox.[1] There is one passage in the letter which must be quoted here. She writes to Mr. Fox to tell him that she has recently become very unhappy because she had begun to entertain doubts

---

[1] This is printed in full in Mr. Conway's *Centenary of the South Place Society*, where (the book being, I believe, still in print) those whom this article may have interested in Sarah Flower may read it.

about the creed in which she has been brought up,
and in which she had hitherto believed. She goes
on to say :

> My mind has been wandering a long time, and now
> it seems to have lost sight of that only invulnerable
> hold against the assaults of this warring world, a firm
> belief in the genuineness of the Scriptures . . . The
> cloud has come over me gradually, and I did not discover
> the darkness in which my soul was shrouded until, in
> seeking to give light to others, my own gloomy state
> became too settled to admit of doubt. It was in
> answering Robert Browning that my mind refused to
> bring forward argument, turned recreant and sided
> with the enemy.

It is, of course, because of its reference to Robert
Browning that I have quoted the above passage.
The young poet was then very much like what Shelley
had been at his age, a very pronounced freethinker,
and one who was eager to make converts to his own
way of thinking. And it was, I believe, Shelley's
' Queen Mab ' which was responsible for Browning's
scepticism. This mood had passed away, it seems,
before the publication of ' Pauline,' in which the poet
expresses his repentance for his youthful errors.

Bertram Dobell.

SONNET

[This sonnet is interesting from its early date, and
from its being the first of Browning's rare contributions
to periodical literature. It was published in Mr. W. J.
Fox's magazine, *The Monthly Repository*, in October
1834, and bears the date of August 17 in that year, with
the signature 'Z.' Browning's subsequent contributions
to this magazine (all with the same signature) were the
song ' A King lived long ago ' (afterwards incorporated
in 'Pippa Passes'), 'Porphyria,' 'Johannes Agricola,' and
the lines, ' Still ailing, wind,' which reappeared in 1864
in ' James Lee's Wife.'

The present sonnet has been reprinted in Edmund
Gosse's ' Personalia ' (1890, pp. 34-35); in the Browning
Society's *Papers*, Part XII.; in Nicoll and Wise's
' Literary Anecdotes,' p. 469; in Hall Griffin and
Minchin's ' Life of Browning ' (1910), p. 306; in the
Cambridge (Boston, U.S.A.) Edition (1895), p. 11; and
in the Centenary Edition of the Poet's Works (1912),
vol. iii. p. 417. The circumstances of its composition
are not known.]

EYES calm beside thee (Lady, could'st thou know!)
  May turn away thick with fast-gathering tears :
I glance not where all gaze : thrilling and low
  Their passionate praises reach thee—my cheek
    wears

Alone no wonder when thou passest by ;
Thy tremulous lids bent and suffused reply
To the irrepressible homage which doth glow
   On every lip but mine : if in thine ears
Their accents linger—and thou dost recall
   Me as I stood, still, guarded, very pale,
Beside each votarist whose lighted brow
Wore worship like an aureole, ' O'er them all
   My beauty,' thou wilt murmur, ' did prevail
Save that one only ' :—Lady, could'st thou know !

   Aug. 17, 1834.

A FOREST THOUGHT [1]

[This early and attractive poem was written on November 4, 1837, on the occasion of Browning standing godfather to the eldest son of his friend William Alexander Dow. He was asked to write something in an album after the christening, and these lines were produced on the spot. The album is still preserved in the family of the poet's friend, but the poem never appeared in print until 1905, when it was published in the periodical *Country Life* (June 10). It was reprinted in ' Robert Browning and Alfred Domett,' 1906, p. xi; in Hall Griffin and Minchin's ' Life,' p. 305 ; and in the Centenary Edition of the Poet's Works, vol. iii. pp. 418–9.

The opening lines are a reminiscence of Browning's visit to Russia in the winter of 1833–4.]

In far Esthonian solitudes

The parent-firs of future woods

Gracefully, airily spire at first

Up to the sky, by the soft sand nurst ;

Self-sufficient are they, and strong

With outspread arms, broad level and long ;

[1] ' Written and inscribed to W. A. and A. D. by their Sincere Friend, Robert Browning, 13 Nelson Sq., November 4, 837.'

But soon in the sunshine and the storm
They darken, changing fast their form—-
Low boughs fall off, and in the bole
Each tree spends all its strenuous soul—-
Till the builder gazes wistfully
Such noble ship-mast wood to see,
And cares not for its soberer hue,
Its rougher bark and leaves more few.

But just when beauty passes away
And you half regret it could not stay,
For all their sap and vigorous life,—
Under the shade, secured from strife
A seedling springs—the forest-tree
In miniature, and again we see
The delicate leaves that will fade one day,
The fan-like shoots that will drop away,
The taper stem a breath could strain—
Which shall foil one day the hurricane :
We turn from this infant of the copse
To the parent-firs,—in their waving tops
To find some trace of the light green tuft
A breath could stir,—in the bole aloft
Column-like set against the sky,
The spire that flourished airily
And the marten bent as she rustled by.

So shall it be, dear Friends, when days
Pass, and in this fair child we trace
Goodness, full-formed in you, tho' dim
Faint-budding, just astir in him :
When rudiments of generous worth
And frankest love in him have birth,
We'll turn to love and worth full-grown,
And learn their fortune from your own.
Nor shall we vainly search to see
His gentleness—simplicity—
Not lost in your maturer grace—
Perfected, but not changing place.

May this grove be a charmed retreat . . .
May northern winds and savage sleet
Leave the good trees untouched, unshorn
A crowning pride of woods unborn :
And gracefully beneath their shield
May the seedling grow !   All pleasures yield
Peace below and peace above,
The glancing squirrels' summer love,
And the brood-song of the cushat-dove !

THE 'MOSES' OF MICHAEL ANGELO

[The MS. of this sonnet by Robert Browning, which he gave to his wife at the time it was written, was discovered lately among some papers of the late Mr. George Smith, his publisher and friend. It is a translation of a sonnet by G. B. F. Zappi, which may be found in A. Rubbi's *Parnaso Italiano*, 1789, tom. 42, p. 162. It was first printed in the *Cornhill Magazine* for September, 1914.]

AND who is He that, sculptured in huge stone,
　　Sitteth a giant, where no works arrive
　　Of straining Art, and hath so prompt and live
The lips, I listen to their very tone ?
Moses is He—Ay, that, makes clearly known
　　The chin's thick boast, and brow's prerogative
　　Of double ray : so did the mountain give
Back to the world that visage, God was grown
Great part of ! Such was he when he suspended
　　Round him the sounding and vast waters ; such
　　When he shut sea on sea o'er Mizraïm.
And ye, his hordes, a vile calf raised, and bended
　　The knee ? This Image had ye raised, not much
　　Had been your error in adoring Him.

　　From Zappi, R. B.　(Given to Ba ' for love's sake,'
Siena.　Sept. 27, '50.)

BEN KARSHOOK'S WISDOM

[This poem, like the last, belongs to the Italian period of Browning's life. It appeared in *The Keepsake* for 1856, with the date, Rome, April 27, 1854, but was not reprinted until it appeared in the first part of the Browning Society's *Papers* in 1881. It has since been reprinted in Mr. W. G. Kingsland's 'Robert Browning, Chief Poet of the Age,' 1890, p. 26; in Mr. W. Sharp's 'Life of Browning,' 1890, p. 167; in Mrs. Orr's 'Life,' 1891 (p. 198 of the edition of 1906); in Nicoll and Wise's 'Literary Anecdotes,' 1895, p. 450; in Hall Griffin and Minchin's 'Life,' p. 307; in the Cambridge (Boston, U.S.A.) Edition (1895), p. 372; and in the Centenary Edition of the Poet's Works, vol. iii. p. 420.

In the poem, 'One Word More,' which forms the epilogue to the 'Men and Women' of 1855, occurred (in the original edition, and in the 'Poetical Works' of 1863 and 1868) the line 'Karshook, Cleon, Norbert and the fifty.' This, however, was a slip of the pen. 'Karshook' cannot have formed one of the fifty when the epilogue was written, less than two months before the publication of the volumes; and in 1881, in reply to an inquiry from Dr. Furnivall, Browning wrote as follows : '*Karshish* is the proper word, referring as it does to him of the "Epistle." *Karshook* (*Heb.* : a Thistle) just belongs to the snarling verses I remember to have written, but forget for whom; the other was the only one of the Fifty' (Wise, 'Letters of Robert Browning,' i. 71). The correction appeared in the Tauchnitz edition of 1872, and in subsequent English editions (certainly from 1879 onwards).]

I

' WOULD a man 'scape the rod ? '
 Rabbi Ben Karshook saith,
' See that he turn to God
 ' The day before his death.'

' Ay, could a man inquire
 ' When it shall come ! ' I say.
The Rabbi's eye shoots fire—
 ' Then let him turn to-day ! '

II

Quoth a young Sadducee :
 ' Reader of many rolls,
' Is it so certain we
 ' Have, as they tell us, souls ? '

' Son, there is no reply ! '
 The Rabbi bit his beard ;
' Certain, a soul have *I*—
 ' *We* may have none,' he sneer'd.

 . . . . .

Thus Karshook, the Hiram's-Hammer,
 The Right-hand Temple-column,
Taught babes in grace their grammar,
 And struck the simple, solemn.

ROME, *April* 27, 1854.

ON BEING DEFIED TO EXPRESS IN A HEXA-
METER :

' YOU OUGHT TO SIT ON THE SAFETY-VALVE '

[The MS. of these Latin hexameters was discovered lately among some papers of the late Mr. George Smith, preserved at Waterloo Place. They were first printed in the *Cornhill Magazine* for September 1914.]

Plane te valvam fas est pressisse salutis :

Æquum est te valvâque, salutis sede, locari :

Convenit in sellâ, valvâ residere salutis,

Omninoque salutis par considere valvâ :

Sedibus est justum valvæ mansisse salutis :

Hæsisse in valvâ te, sede salutis, oportet :

Est tibi valvis, inque salutis sede, sedendum :

Valvâ, sede salutiferâ super, assidet omnis

Qui discrimen adit, fortem quem numina servant :

Multiplicem versum tu mente, Robertule, figas !

Feb. 22, '66.

LINES TO THE MEMORY OF HIS
PARENTS (1866)

[These lines by Robert Browning, addressed apparently to the memory of his parents—from a MS. in the
handwriting of Miss Browning—were among the papers
disposed of at the Browning Sale in May 1913. They
were probably written in 1866, the year of his father's
death. They were first printed in the *Cornhill Magazine*,
February 1914.]

' WORDS I might else have been compelled to say
   In silence to my heart,—great love, great praise
   Of thee, my Father—have been freely said
   By those whom none shall blame ; and while thy
         life
   Endures, a beauteous thing, in their record
   I may desist ; but thou art not alone :
   They lie beside thee whom thou lovest most ;
   Soft sanctuary-tapers of thy house,
   Close-curtained when the Priest came forth,—on
         these
    Let peace be, peace on thee, my Mother, too !
   The child that never knew you, and the Girl
   In whom your gentle souls seemed born again
   To bless us longer. Peace like yours be mine
   Till the same quiet home receive us all.'

A ROUND ROBIN

(Written by Robert Browning and sent to Miss Harriet Hosmer in Rome.)

[Browning and his sister were staying in Scotland with Lady Ashburton ; other members of the party were the Storys, Lady Marian Alford, and Sir Roderick Murchison. Miss Harriet Hosmer, an American sculptress of considerable repute, with a studio in Rome, had associated with the Brownings both in Florence and in Rome. The lines were first printed in ' Harriet Hosmer, Letters and Memories,' edited by Cornelia Carr (John Lane, 1913), pp. 275–6.]

Loch Luichart, Dingwall, N.B.

DEAR HOSMER ; or still dearer, Hatty—
Mixture of *miele* and of *latte*,
So good and sweet and—somewhat fatty—

Why linger still in Rome's old glory
When Scotland lies in cool before ye ?
Make haste and come !—quoth Mr. Story.

Sculpture is not a thing to sit to
In summertime ; do find a fit toe
To kick the clay aside a bit—oh,
Yield to our prayers ! quoth Mrs. Ditto.

Give comfort to us poor and needy
Who, wanting you, are waiting greedy
Our meat and drink, yourself, quoth Edie.

Nay, though, past clay, you chip the Parian,
Throw chisel down ! quoth Lady Marian.

Be welcome, as to cow—the fodder-rick !
Excuse the simile !—quoth Sir Roderick.

Say not (in Scotch) ' in troth it canna be '—
But, honey, milk and, indeed, manna be !
Forgive a stranger !—Sarianna B.

Don't set an old acquaintance frowning,
But come and quickly ! quoth R. Browning,
For since prodigious fault is found with you,
I—that is, Robin—must be Round with you.

PS. Do wash your hands, or leave the dirt on,
     But leave the tool as Gammer Gurton
     Her needle lost,—Lady Ashburton.
     Thus ends this letter—ease my sick heart,
     And come to my divine Loch Luichart !

                     W. W. STORY, his mark X,
                     EMELYN STORY,
                     EDITH MARION STORY,
Signatures of : In M. ALFORD,
order of infraposi-   RODERICK MURCHISON,
tion, I am,   SARIANNA BROWNING,
                     ROBERT BROWNING,
                     L. ASHBURTON.

     Sept. 5, 1869.

HELEN'S TOWER

(Written at the request of the Marquis of Dufferin)

[This sonnet was written as far back as 1870, but was not published until it appeared in the *Pall Mall Gazette*, on December 28, 1883. It was written at the invitation of Lord Dufferin, for the tower which he built at Clandeboye in memory of his mother, Helen, Countess of Gifford, and bears the date of April 26, 1870. Tennyson's lines on the same occasion are printed in his ' Tiresias and other Poems ' (1885). It is strange that Browning should not have included so fine a poem in any of his subsequent volumes.

It was reprinted in the Browning Society's *Papers* ; in Nicoll and Wise's ' Literary Anecdotes of the Nineteenth Century,' vol. i. (1895); in the Cambridge (Boston U.S.A.) Edition (1895), p. 601; and in the Centenary Edition of the Poet's Works, vol. ix. p. 348.]

WHO hears of Helen's Tower, may dream perchance
  How the Greek beauty from the Scaean gate
  Gazed on old friends unanimous in hate,
Death-doom'd because of her fair countenance.
Hearts would leap otherwise at thy advance,
  Lady, to whom this tower is consecrate !
  Like hers, thy face once made all eyes elate,
Yet, unlike hers, was bless'd by every glance.

D

The Tower of Hate is outworn, far and strange :
  A transitory shame of long ago,
  It dies into the sand from which it sprang ;
But thine, Love's rock-built Tower, shall fear no
    change :
  God's self laid stable earth's foundations so,
  When all the morning stars together sang.

  April 26, 1870.

.

'OH LOVE, LOVE'

[The following lines are a translation of Euripides'
'Hippolytus,' ll. 525–544, and were contributed by
Browning to a little handbook on the Greek poet by
Professor J. P. Mahaffy, in 1879. They have been re-
printed in the Browning Society's *Papers*, 1881, Pt. I.
p. 69 ; in Nicoll and Wise's ' Literary Anecdotes of the
Nineteenth Century,' vol. i. (1895) ; in the Cambridge
(Boston, U.S.A.) Edition (1895), p. 874 ; and in the
Centenary Edition of the Poet's Works, vol. ix. p. 345.]

Oh Love, Love, thou that from the eyes diffusest
Yearning, and on the soul sweet grace inducest—
Souls against whom thy hostile march is made—
Never to me be manifest in ire,
Nor, out of time and tune, my peace invade !
Since neither from the fire—
No, nor the stars—is launched a bolt more mighty
Than that of Aphrodité
Hurled from the hands of Love, the boy with Zeus
    for sire.

Idly, how idly, by the Alpheian river
And in the Pythian shrines of Phœbus, quiver
Blood-offerings from the bull, which Hellas heaps :
While Love we worship not—the Lord of men !
Worship not him, the very key who keeps
Of Aphrodité, when
She closes up her dearest chamber-portals :
—Love, when he comes to mortals,
Wide-wasting, through those deeps of woes beyond
    the deep.

VERSES FROM ' THE HOUR WILL COME '

[These lines are a translation of a poem in a German tale entitled ' The Hour will Come,' by Wilhelmine von Hillern. An English version of it was made by Miss Clara Bell, which appeared in 1879 ; and for this Browning's lines were written. His name was not attached to the translation, but acknowledgments are made ' to the kindness of a friend.'

The poem has been reprinted in the *Whitehall Review*, March 1, 1883 ; in the Browning Society's *Papers* ; in Nicoll and Wise's ' Literary Anecdotes of the Nineteenth Century,' vol. i. (1895) ; in the Cambridge (Boston, U.S.A.) Edition (1895), p. 910, and in the Centenary Edition of the Poet's Works, vol. ix. p. 346.]

THE blind man to the maiden said,
   ' O thou of hearts the truest,
Thy countenance is hid from me ;
Let not my question anger thee !
   Speak, though in words the fewest.

' Tell me, what kind of eyes are thine ?
   Dark eyes, or light ones rather ? '
' My eyes are a decided brown—
So much at least, by looking down,
   From the brook's glass I gather.'

' And is it red—thy little mouth ?
　That too the blind must care for.'
' Ah ! I would tell it soon to thee,
Only—none yet has told it me,
　I cannot answer, therefore.

' But dost thou ask what heart I have—
　There hesitate I never.
In thine own breast 't is borne, and so
'T is thine in weal, and thine in woe,
　For life, for death—thine ever ! '

TRANSLATION FROM PINDAR'S SEVENTH
OLYMPIAN, EPODE III.

[The following draft letter and poem, found among
the poet's papers, were sold with the Browning Collections in 1913. Although addressed to the Editor
of the *Pall Mall Gazette*, the letter appears not to have
been sent ; in any case, a search through the file of the
paper about that time does not reveal its publication. In
December of the same year, however, the editor printed
no less than three poems by Browning : the sonnet
on 'Goldoni,' some lines from Horace (' On Singers '),
and the important poem ' Helen's Tower,' all given in
this volume. This is one of many instances showing
that the poet loved to exercise his masterly knowledge
of the classics. The occasion was an incident in the
celebrated trial 'Belt *v.* Lawes,' when the Judge, on the
strength of a passage in Aristotle, intimated that a
Middlesex jury was as good a judge of Art as a Royal
Academician.]

(19 Warwick Crescent, W.)
Jan. 14, '83.

Letter to ' Pall Mall Gazette.'

SIR,—We have recently been favoured with a Greek
quotation,—warranted however rather by the bench
than the Book-$\left\{\begin{array}{l}\text{case}\\\text{shelf}\end{array}\right\}$—on the subject of Art.
Another one, as apposite, might be made from another

old authority; and, curiously enough, it immediately precedes the passage which was illustrated, some years ago, by one of the finest pictures of the President. For the general reader, I venture a rough version : the Middlesex Jury needs no reminding that the original occurs in Pindar's Seventh Olympian, Epode III.

I am, Sir, Yours obediently,

R. B.

The Editor of the *Pall Mall Gazette*.

AND to these Rhodians she, the sharp eyed one,
  Gave the supremacy, in every art,—
  And, nobly-labouring play the craftsman's part
Beyond all dwellers underneath the sun.
So that the very ways by which ye pass
  Bore sculpture, living things that walk or creep
  Like as the life : whence very high and deep
Indeed the glory of the artist was.
For, in the well-instructed artist, skill,
However great, receives our greeting,
As something greater still,
When unaccompanied by cheating.

SONNET TO RAWDON BROWN

[Rawdon Brown was, as indicated in this sonnet, an Englishman. Visiting Venice temporarily, he remained for forty years, and died there in 1883. He is mentioned in travel books as having a very perfect knowledge of the city. Toni was his gondolier. The epitaph on his tomb is taken from the third and fourth lines. The sonnet was first printed in the *Century Magazine*, February 1884, vol. xxvii. p. 640 ; being reprinted in the Browning Society's *Papers*, 1884, Pt. V. p. 132 ; and in the Cambridge (Boston, U.S.A.) Edition of the Poet's Works (1895), p. 947.]

SIGHED Rawdon Brown : ' Yes, I'm departing,
    Toni !
I needs must, just this once before I die,
Revisit England : *Anglus* Brown am I,
Although my heart's Venetian. Yes, old crony—
Venice and London—London's " Death the bony "
Compared with Life—that's Venice ! What a sky,
A sea, this morning ! One last look ! Good-by,
Cà Pesaro ! No lion—I'm a coney
To weep ! I'm dazzled ; 't is that sun I view

Rippling the . . . the . . . *Cospetto*, Toni !   Down
With carpet-bag, and off with valise-straps !
Bella Venezia, non ti lascio più ! '
Nor did Brown ever leave her : well, perhaps
Browning, next week, may find himself quite Brown !

    Nov. 28, 1883.

GOLDONI

[The origin of the Goldoni sonnet is given by the poet himself in a letter to Dr. Furnivall of December 3, 1883 (Wise, ' Letters of R. Browning,' ii. 31) :

' They are going to unveil and display here a monument erected to Goldoni, and the committee did me the honour to request a word or two for insertion in an Album to which the principal men of letters in Italy have contributed. I made a sonnet, which they please to think so well of that they preface the work with it.'

Mrs. Bronson (*Cornhill Magazine*, February 1902, p. 10) adds that the sonnet was written very rapidly, and only two or three trifling alterations were made in the original copy.

The sonnet was printed in the *Pall Mall Gazette*, December 8, 1883, and has since been reprinted in the Browning Society's *Papers*, 1884, Pt. V. p. 99 ; in Nicoll and Wise's 'Literary Anecdotes of the Nineteenth Century,' vol. i. (1895); in the Cambridge (Boston, U.S.A.) Edition (1895), p. 910 ; and in the Centenary Edition of the Poet's Works, vol. ix. p. 347.]

GOLDONI—good, gay, sunniest of souls—

Glassing half Venice in that verse of thine—

What though it just reflect the shade and shine

Of common life, nor render, as it rolls,

Grandeur and gloom ?   Sufficient for thy shoals
  Was Carnival : Parini's depths enshrine
  Secrets unsuited to that opaline
Surface of things which laughs along thy scrolls.
There throng the people : how they come and go,
  Lisp the soft language, flaunt the bright garb—see—
On Piazza, Calle, under Portico
  And over Bridge !   Dear king of Comedy,
Be honoured !   Thou that didst love Venice so,
  Venice, and we who love her, all love thee.

ON SINGERS

[First printed in the *Pall Mall Gazette*, December 13, 1883, and reprinted in the Browning Society's *Papers*, 1884, Pt. V. p. 99. Robert Browning was asked to write in a lady's album, where he saw some one had written the lines from Horace] :

OMNIBUS hoc vitium est cantoribus, inter amicos
Ut nunquam inducant animum cantare rogati,
Injussi nunquam desistant.

He immediately appended the following translation :

All singers, trust me, have this common vice,
To sing 'mid friends you'll have to ask them twice.
If you don't ask them 't is another thing,
Until the judgment-day be sure they'll sing.

GEROUSIOS OINOS

[This poem, which was put into type at the same time as the volume ' Jocoseria ' (1883), was not eventually published, but came to light in its present form as a rough printed proof in what is known as ' galley-slip ' among the poet's papers offered at the sale of the Browning Collections in May 1913, and purchased by the well-known bibliophile, Mr. Bertram Dobell. It was first published in the *Cornhill Magazine* and the *Century Magazine*, April 1914.]

I DREAMED there was once held a feast :
That lords assembled, most and least,
   And set them down to dine ;
Till, eating ended—high of heart
Each guest,— the butler did his part,
   Poured out their proper wine.

Good tipple and of various growth
(You may believe without an oath)
   Glorified every glass :
All drank in honour of the host,
Then—high of heart,—rose least and most,
   And left the room—alas.

For in rushed straightway loon and lout,
Mere servingmen who skulked without :
   ' Our masters turn their backs,
And now's the time to taste and try
What meat lords munch,—and, by and by,
   What wine they swill—best smacks.'

So said, so done : first, hunger spends
Its rage on victual, odds and ends :
   But seeing that rage appeased,
' Now for the lords' wine,' all agree,
' Kept from the like of you and me !
   Wet whistles, chins once greased !

' How ! not content with loading crop,
These lords have scarcely left a drop
   In every glass deep-drained !
The niggards mean our feast to prove
A horse-regale ! But, one remove
   From wine is water stained.

' Fill up each glass with water ! Get
Such flavour as may stick fast yet,
   Fancy shall do the rest !
Besides we boast our private flasks,
Good stiff mundungus, home-brewed casks
   Beating their bottled best !

'So here's your health to watered port !
Thanks : mine is sherry of a sort.
   Claret, though thinnish, clear.
My Burgundy's the genuine stuff—
Bettered and bittered just enough
   By mixing it with beer.'

Oh, England (I awoke and laughed)
True wine thy lordly Poets quaffed,
   Yet left,—for, what cared they !—
Each glass its heel-tap—flavouring sup
For flunkeys when, to liquor up,
   In swarmed—who, need I say !

THE FOUNDER OF THE FEAST

(*To Arthur Chappell*)

[In 1884 Browning contributed these lines to the Album presented to Mr. Arthur Chappell, the organiser of the Popular Concerts at St. James's Hall, thus testifying to his love of music and to his frequent attendance at concerts. The poem was printed in *The World* for April 16, 1884, and has been reprinted in the Browning Society's *Papers*, 1884, Pt. VII. p. 18; in Nicoll and Wise's 'Literary Anecdotes of the Nineteenth Century,' vol. i. (1895); in the Cambridge (Boston, U.S.A.) Edition (1895), p. 947, and in the Centenary Edition of the Poet's Works (1912), vol. ix. p. 349. It has hitherto contained fifteen lines, but the following version, reduced to the sonnet form of fourteen lines (by the deletion of line nine and the consequent revision of line ten), is printed from a cutting taken from the *World* and corrected by Browning, which was found among his papers.]

' ENTER my palace,' if a prince should say—

   ' Feast with the Painters ! See, in bounteous row,

   They range from Titian up to Angelo ! '

Could we be silent at the rich survey ?

E

A host so kindly, in as great a way
   Invites to banquet, substitutes for show
   Sound that's diviner still, and bids us know
Bach like Beethoven ; are we thankless, pray ?
   To him whose every guest not idly vaunts,
   ' Sense has received the utmost Nature grants,
My cup was filled with rapture to the brim,
   When, night by night—ah, memory, how it
      haunts !—
   Music was poured by perfect ministrants,
By Hallè, Schumann, Piatti, Joachim.'

  April 5, 1884.

THE NAMES

(To Shakespeare)

[Written for the ' Shaksperean Show-Book' published
in May 1884, in connection with the Shaksperean Show
held at the Albert Hall in aid of the Hospital for Women
in the Fulham Road. It was reprinted in the *Pall
Mall Gazette* for May 29 ; in the Browning Society's
Papers, 1884, Pt. V. p. 105 ; in Nicoll and Wise's
' Literary Anecdotes of the Nineteenth Century,' vol. i.
(1895) ; in the Cambridge (Boston, U.S.A.) Edition
(1895), p. 947 ; and in the Centenary Edition of the
Poet's Works (1912), vol. ix. p. 350.]

SHAKESPEARE !—to such name's sounding what
    succeeds

  Fitly as silence ? Falter forth the spell,—

  Act follows word, the speaker knows full well,

Nor tampers with its magic more than needs.

Two names there are : That which the Hebrew
    reads

  With his soul only : if from lips it fell,

  Echo, back thundered by earth, heaven and hell,

E 2

Would own ' Thou did'st create us ! ' Nought impedes
We voice the other name, man's most of might,
   Awesomely, lovingly : let awe and love
Mutely await their working, leave to sight
   All of the issue as—below—above—
Shakespeare's creation rises : one remove,
Though dread—this finite from that infinite

WHY I AM A LIBERAL

[Browning never took an active part in politics, and
this statement of his political faith, composed in response
to an invitation from Mr. Andrew Reid, and published
by him in a volume with the same title issued in 1885
in support of the then waning Liberal cause, appeared
only a few months before he ceased to support the
official Liberal party. The principles expressed in it,
however, had no reference to the temporary policies of
any party, and remained his principles to the end of
his life.

The lines were reprinted in the Browning Society's
Papers, 1885, p. 89; in ' Sonnets of the Century,' edited
by W. Sharp (1886) ; in Nicoll and Wise's ' Literary
Anecdotes of the Nineteenth Century,' vol. i. (1895) ; in
the Cambridge (Boston, U.S.A.) Edition (1895), p. 948 ;
and in the Centenary Edition of the Poet's Works
(1912), vol. ix. p. 351.]

' WHY ? ' Because all I haply can and do,
    All that I am now, all I hope to be—
    Whence comes it save from fortune setting free
Body and soul the purpose to pursue,
God traced for both ? If fetters, not a few,
    Of prejudice, convention, fall from me,
    These shall I bid men—each in his degree
Also God-guided—bear, and gaily too ?

But little do or can the best of us :
    That little is achieved through Liberty.
Who, then, dares hold—emancipated thus—
    His fellow shall continue bound ? Not I
Who live, love, labour freely, nor discuss
    A brother's right to freedom. That is ' Why.'

LINES FOR THE TOMB OF LEVI LINCOLN THAXTER

[Mr. Thaxter, who was born at Waterford in Massachusetts in 1824 and died in 1884, was an enthusiastic student of Browning's poems, and in his later years gave readings from the poet's works. These lines have been printed in Mrs. Orr's *Life*, 1908, p. 335, and in the Cambridge (Boston, U.S.A.) Edition (1895), p. 948.]

THOU, whom these eyes saw never,—Say friends
    true
Who say my soul, helped onward by my song,
Though all unwittingly, has helped thee too ?
I gave but of the little that I knew :
How were the gift requited, while along
Life's path I pace, couldst thou make weakness
    strong,
Help me with knowledge—for Life's Old—Death's
    New !

    R. B. to L. L. T., *April* 19, 1885.

EPPS

As far as can now be recollected, it was about the year 1884 that Robert Browning announced to Mrs. Edmund Gosse and Lady Alma-Tadema, whose maiden name was Epps, that he was proposing to write a poem about their ' Kentish ancestor.' They were not aware of any relationship with the hero, but Browning laughingly insisted that they must not throw any doubt upon the fact, because he proposed to endow them with this ' ancestor.' Shortly afterwards he showed them the MS. of the verses, which he did not treat as a serious specimen of his poetic art. It is not recollected what became of the MS., of which the ladies kept no copy ; it was doubtless returned to Mr. Browning.

EDMUND GOSSE.

January 12, 1914.

[The MS. was included in the sale of the Browning Collections in 1913. The poem was first printed in the *Cornhill Magazine* and the *New York Outlook*, October 1913. As a result of that publication, Mr. Edmund Gosse has very kindly given the above interesting facts in connection with this characteristic historical poem.]

Asks anyone—' Where's a tag for *steps* ? '
  I answer—' Waiting its time
Till somebody versed in the English tongue
Shall start at the challenge, cry " unsung
  Till now, and all for want of a rhyme,
Is the prowess of Kentish Epps ? " '

Two hundred and eighty years ago
  Befell the siege of Ostend ;
Epps soldiered it there : and, hew or hack
At his breast as the enemy might, his back
  Got never a scratch : yet life must end
Somehow,—Epps ended—so !

He had lost an eye on the walls, look out
  No longer could Epps : said he—
' Give me Saint George's cross—our flag
To carry : I can't see them—foes brag :
  At all events they shall soon see me,
Knight and knave, lord and lout ! '

' Epps got loose again ! ' yelped the curs :
  ' At him—the blind side best !
Together as one—in rush, on a heap,
Buffet the old maiméd bull ! Fame's cheap
  This morn for whoso has mind to wrest
Yon flag from his hold, win spurs ! '

As a big wave bursts on a rock, broke they
   On bannerman Epps : as staunch
The drowned rock stands, but emerging feels
Weeds late on its head lie loose at its heels,
   So left bare, swirl-stript, root and branch,

Of his $\left\{ \begin{array}{l} \text{band} \\ \text{company} \end{array} \right\}$ stood—Epps laughed gay :

' I with my flag—that's well, no fear
   The colours stick to the staff :
But the staff 'tis a mere hand holds—lets fall
If there stab me or shoot one knave of them all :
   To hinder which game—' I hear Epps laugh—
' Stick, flag, to a new staff—here ! '

And off in a trice from the staff that's wood,
   And on to a staff that's flesh,

Tears Epps and $\left\{ \begin{array}{l} \text{ties} \\ \text{binds} \end{array} \right\}$ me $\left\{ \begin{array}{l} \text{round} \\ \text{tight} \end{array} \right\}$ about his breast
The flag in a red swathe : ' Here's the vest
   For my lifelong wear ; at the foe afresh !
Flagstaff, show your hardihood ! '

Whereat, in a twinkling, man and horse
   Went down—one, two and three,

And how many more ?   But they shot and slashed
Two $\begin{Bmatrix} \text{bullets} \\ \text{balls} \end{Bmatrix}$ have riddled, two sword-blades gashed
  The staff through the flag,—$\begin{Bmatrix} \text{leave} \\ \text{left} \end{Bmatrix}$ free
To despoilers,—you think,—a corse ?

No !   Back from his slayers, staggeringly
  But, staff-like, stout to the last,
Up to his mates—of the checked advance—
Reels Epps, his soul in his countenance,
  As he falters ' See !   Flag to the staff sticks fast,
And, flag saved, staff may die ! '

And die did Epps, with his English round :
  Not so the fame of the feat :
For Donne and Dekker, brave poets and rare,
Gave it honour and praise : and I join the pair
  With heart that's loud though my voice compete
As a pipe with their trumpet-sound !

  January 6, 1886.

THE ISLE'S ENCHANTRESS

[Lines, on Felix Moscheles' painting called ' The
Isle's Enchantress,' given by Robert Browning to the
painter and printed in the *Pall Mall Gazette* by the poet's
permission.—*March* 26, 1889.]

WIND wafted from the sunset, o'er the swell
Of summer's slumbrous sea, herself asleep
Come shoreward, in her iridescent shell
Cradled, the isle's enchantress. You who keep
A drowsy watch beside her,—watch her well !

UNFINISHED DRAFT OF A POEM WHICH MAY
BE ENTITLED ' ÆSCHYLUS' SOLILOQUY '

[At the sale of the Browning MSS. on May 2, 1913,
this MS. was catalogued as :

> Lot 188.   Browning (R.) Auto. Draft of a poem.
> in blank verse, 4 pp. 8vo., unfinished and perhaps
> unpublished, apparently intended for ' Aristo-
> phanes' Apology,' but not used, beginning :
>
> > ' I am an old and solitary man.'

This description is correct in that the poem had never
been published, but it is evident that it was not a draft
for ' Aristophanes' Apology,' but a soliloquy of the aged
Æschylus, just before the prophecy as to his death was
fulfilled by an eagle dropping a tortoise upon his head.
The poem was first printed in the *Cornhill Magazine*
and the *New York Independent*, November 1913, strictly
according to the original MS., now in the British
Museum, as it reads with the poet's variants and
queries.   In line 56 ' Dephos' is obviously a slip of the
pen for ' Delphos,' and in line 59 ' rush ' seems the
best interpretation of a scarcely legible word, of which
the MS. contains many.]

I AM an old and solitary man
And now at set of sun in Sicily
I sit down in the middle of this plain
Which drives between the mountains and the sea
Its blank of nature.   If a traveller came

Seeing my bare bald skull and_my still brows
And massive features coloured to a stone
The tragic mask of a humanity
Whose part is played to an end,—he might mistake me
For some god Terminus set on these flats
Or broken marble Faunus.   Let it be.
Life has ebbed from me—I am on dry ground—
All sounds of life I held so thunderous sweet
Shade off to silence—all the perfect shapes
Born of perception and men's images (imagery ?)
Which thronged against the outer rim of earth
And hung with floating faces over it
Grow dim and dimmer—all the motions drawn
From Beauty in action which spun audibly
My brain round in a rapture, have grown still.
There's a gap 'twixt me and the life once mine,
Now others' and not mine, which now roars off
In gradual declination—till at last
I hear it in the distance droning small
Like a bee at sunset.   Ay, and that bee's hum
The buzzing fly and mouthing of the grass
Cropped slowly near me by some straying sheep
Are strange to me with life—and separate from me
The outside of my being—I myself
Grow to silence, fasten to the calm
Of inorganic nature . . . sky and rocks—

I shall pass on into their unity
When dying down into impersonal dusk.
      Ah, ha—these flats are wide !
The prophecy which said the house would fall
And thereby crush me, must bring down the sky
The only roof above me where I sit
Or ere it prove its oracle to-day.
Stand fast ye pillars of the constant Heavens
As Life doth in me—I who did not die
That day in Athens when the people's scorn
Hissed toward the sun as if to darken it
Because my thoughts burned too much for the eyes
Over my head, because I spoke my Greek
Too deep down in my soul to suit their case.
Who did not die to see the solemn vests
Of my white chorus round the thymele
Flutter like doves, and sweep back like a cloud
Before the shrill lipped people . . . but stood calm
And cold, and felt the theatre wax hot
With mouthing whispers . . . the man Æschylus
Is gray I fancy—and his wrinkles ridge
The smoothest of his phrases—or the times
Have grown too polished for this old rough work—
We have no Sphynxes in the Parthenon
Nor any flints at Dephos—or forsooth,
I think the Sphynxes wrote this Attic Greek—

Our Sophocles hath something more than this
Cast out on—and their smile——I would not die (?)
At this time by the crushing of a house
Who lived that Day out . . . I would go to death
With voluntary and majestic steps
Jove thundering on the right hand.   Let it be.

I am an old and solitary man
Mine eyes feel dimly out the setting sun
Which drops its great red fruit of bitterness
To-day as other days, as every day
Within the patient waters.   What do I say ?
I whistle out my scorn against the sun
Who (knell) his trilogy morn noon and night
And set this tragic world against the sun—
Forgive me, great Apollo.—Bitter fruit
I think we never found that holy sun
Or ere with conjurations of our hands
Drove up the saltness of our hearts to it
A blessed fruit, a full Hesperian fruit
Which the fair sisters with their starry eyes
Did warm to scarlet bloom.   O holy sun
My eyes are weak and cannot hold thee round !
But in my large soul there is room for thee—
All human wrongs and shames cast out from it,—
And I invite thee, sun, to sphere thyself

In my large soul, and let my thoughts in white
Keep chorus round thy glory—Oh the days
In which I sate upon Hymettus hill
Ilissus seeming louder : and the groves
Of blessed olive thinking of their use
A little tunicked child and felt my thoughts   (?)
Rise past the golden bees against thy face
Great sun upon the sea.   The city lay
Beneath me like an eaglet in an egg,
The beak and claws shut whitely up in calm—
And calm were the great waters—and the hills
Holding at arm's length their unmolten snows
Plunged in the light of heaven which trickled back
On all sides, a libation to the world.
                 There I sate a child
Half hidden in purple thyme with knees drawn up
By clasping of my little arms, and cheek
Laid slant across them with obtruded nose
And full eyes gazing . . . ay, my eyes climbed up
Against the heated metal of thy shield
Till their persistent look clove through the fire
And struck it into manyfolded fires   (?)
And opened out the secret of the night
Hid in the day-source Darkness mixed with light.
Then shot innumerous arrows in my eyes
From all sides of the Heavens—so blinding me—

F

As countless as the norland snowflakes fall
Before the north winds—rapid, wonderful,
Some shafts as bright as sun rays nine times drawn
Thro' the heart of the sun—some black as night in
    Hell—
All mixed, sharp, driven against me ! and as I gazed
(For I gazed still) I saw the sea and earth
Leap up as wounded by the innumerous shafts
And hurry round, and whirl into a blot
Across which evermore fell thick the shafts
As norland snow falls thick before the wind (? flakes
    fall)
Until the northmen at the cavern's mouth
Can see no pine tree through.   I could see nought
No earth, no sea, no sky, no sun itself,
Only that arrowy rush of black and white
Across a surf of rainbows infinite

Drove $\begin{cases} \text{piercing ? ?} \\ \text{pressing ?} \end{cases}$ and blinding and astonishing

And through it all Homerus the blind man
Did chant his vowelled music in my brain.
And then it was revealed, it was revealed
That I should be a priest of the Unseen
And build a bridge of sounds across the straight
From Heaven to earth whence all the Gods might
    walk

Nor bend it with their soles (?)
And then I saw the Gods tread past me slow
From out the portals of the hungry dark
And each one as he past, breathed in my face
And made me greater—First old Saturn came
Blind with eternal watches—calm and blind—
Then Zeus—his eagle blinking on his wrist ⎱
To his hand's rod of fires—in thunder rolls ⎰ ?
He glode on grandly—While the troop of Prayers
Buzzed dimly in the ⎱mist ⎰ of his light
⎰shadow⎱
With murmurous sounds, and poor beseeching tears.
And Neptune with beard and locks drawn straight
As seaweed—ay and Pluto with his Dark
Cutting the dark as Lightning cuts the sun
Made individual by intensity.
And then Apollo trenching on the dusk
With a white glory, while the lute he bore
Struck on the air

JOAN OF ARC AND THE KINGFISHER

[This and the following ten fragments of verse are
from MSS. in the autograph of Robert Browning which
were included in the sale of the Browning Collections
in 1913. They are now printed for the first time, and
they may be said to reveal the poet in historical, social,
and humorous moods.   The following lines were written
as a motto for a picture painted by his son.]

Now, as she fain would bathe, one eventide,
—God's Maid, this Joan—from a pool's edge she
    spied
That fair blue bird clowns call the Fisher King :
And ' 'Las,' sighed she, ' my Liege is such a thing
As thou, lord but of one poor lonely place
Out of his whole wide France : were mine the grace
To set my Dauphin free as thou, blue bird ! '

                 ' Joan of Arc,' Canto I.

A SCENE IN THE BUILDING OF THE INQUISITORS AT ANTWERP

[Probably, like the last, a motto for a picture by his son.]

THEREFORE the hand of God
Thy sentence with His finger
Hath written, and this tribunal
Consigneth it now straightway
Unto·the secular arm.

REPLY TO A TELEGRAPHIC GREETING

BANCROFT, the message-bearing wire
Which flashes thy ' All Hail ' to-day,
Moves slowlier than my heart's desire
That, half what pen writes, tongue might‾say.

REPLIES TO CHALLENGES TO RHYME

IF ever you meet a rhinoceros
And a tree be in sight,
Climb quick! for his might
Is a match for the gods : he could toss Eros!

HANG your kickshaws and your made-dishes
Give me bread and cheese and radishes—
Even stalish bread and baddish cheese.

YOU may at Pekin as at Poggibonsi,
Instead of tricksy priest, a dodgy bonze see.

AH, massa! such a fiery oss
As him I rode at Timbuctoo!
Him would not suit a quiet boss!
Him kick, him rear, and him buck too!

VENUS, sea froth's child,
Playing old gooseberry,
Marries Lord Rosebery [1]
To Miss de Rothschild ! [2]

' HORNS make the buck ' cried rash Burdett ;
And then used speech befitting Timbuctoo :
' I would the horns of the creature met
I' the belly o' the king and so made him buck
    too ! '

DIALOGUE BETWEEN FATHER AND DAUGHTER

F. Then, what do you say to the poem of Mizpah ?
D. An out and out masterpiece—that's what it
    is, Pa !

[1] The marriage took place in 1878.
[2] Hannah, only daughter and heiress of Baron Meyer de Rothschild, died 1890.

THE DOGMA TRIUMPHANT

Epigram on the Voluntary Imprisonment of the Pope as proving his infallibility.

DEAR HERRIES, let's hope, by impounding your Pope,
  We prove him infallible : *quare ?*
Why, if he's in durance, who'll have the assurance
  To hint ' *Papa potest errare* '?

ITALIA.

POEMS BY
ELIZABETH BARRETT BROWNING

Elizabeth Barrett Browning

from a miniature painting, kindly lent by Miss E. Murray Smith

THE ENCHANTRESS

[Mrs. Browning was always diffident, and perhaps over-scrupulous, in the selection of her poetry for publication. Her anxiety was to publish only of her best, and she displayed rare discrimination and care in her choice. Much of her earlier work, therefore, as was revealed at the dispersal of the Browning Collections in 1913, remained in MS. unpublished.

The following five poems, written during the years 1830 to 1839, are representative of this new material. They must have been purposely withheld from the various volumes of verse prepared for press by their author between the years 1833 and 1850.

The dates of composition of ' The Enchantress ' and ' Leila : a Tale ' are not definitely known, but both were probably written in the early 'thirties of the last century. The former is apparently an unfinished poem. The verses entitled ' Epistle to a Canary ' (1837), to which Mr. Edmund Gosse has prefixed an illuminating account, would naturally have been regarded by Mrs. Browning as of too intimate and personal a character for publication at that time.

Of these five poems, the MSS. of the first four were acquired by Mr. Thomas J. Wise for his renowned collection ; and he has printed thirty copies of each of them in his series of booklets issued for private circulation, as follows :—

'Epistle to a Canary,' 1837.　By Elizabeth Barrett Barrett.　Edited by Edmund Gosse, C.B.　19 pp. London, 1913 (reprinted in the *Cornhill Magazine*, June 1914).

'The Enchantress and other Poems.'　By Elizabeth Barrett Browning.　28 pp., London (1913).

['The Enchantress.'　pp. 7-11.

'A True Dream.'　pp. 12-18 (reprinted in the *Cornhill Magazine*, July 1914).]

'Leila : A Tale.'　By Elizabeth Barrett Browning. 35 pp.　London (1913).

The MS. of 'Epistle to a Canary' is now in the collection of Mr. Edmund Gosse.]

THE ENCHANTRESS

I

ABOVE the Aegean wave, the sun is glancing
　And o'er the dark depths, gently, silently
The flitting lights, in rainbow hues, are dancing
　In rippling melody, the waters sigh,
And the soft breathing zephyrs give reply.
　Oh ! beautiful is morn, and sweetly play
The light and shadows o'er that lurid sky,
　As the last cloud fades tranquilly away,
　　And the young hours unclose the roseate lids of day.

II

Sweet is the musical breath of perfumed even,
   And sweet her setting sun on blushing wave,
Hope's death bed, where we catch a glimpse of Heaven
   Which smiles on death, and triumphs o'er the grave.
Sweet are her silvery tides that calmly lave
   The soft ascent of those delightful shores,
When zephyrs kiss each other, and enslave
     Their wings in sunbeam chains and wreathed
       flowers,
     But sweeter, holier far, the morning's ambient
       hours.

III

A little bark is sleeping on the billow,
   And round its stern the harmless breezes play,
Cradling its frail form on a faithless pillow.
   Now Judas-like the light, quick, sparkling spray
Kisses the prow, as onwards shoots its way
   Cutting with flashing keel the silver tide,
And now impetuous through the quiet bay
   It seems on wings of life and light to glide,
   Till on the pebbly shore it heaves its grating side.

IV

And from the stern a laughing maiden leapt,
  And lightly on the golden sand she sprung ;
The waving ringlets from her fair brow swept
  With snowy fingers playfully she wrung
From the wet spray.   Then all around her flung
  A glance of hasty, anxious tenderness ;
Paused, looked again, and somewhat wildly sung
  A little air, then mute and motionless
  Hung on the gale which seemed like one dear voice
    to bless.

V

Like the conception of a Poet's dream
  Upon the wings of Inspiration caught,
So exquisite in beauty, we might deem
  That spiritual essence in her form was wrought
Purer than fancy, lovelier than thought.
  From the deep azure of her eye of light
The young soul seemed to spring untamed, untaught ;
  And laughing from its casement pure and bright
  Breathe through the o'ershadowing lash to care
    a long good night.

VI

From brow of purest marble gracefully
  Fell the bright locks upon her shoulder fair,
Like moonbeams sleeping on a quiet sea.
  Thou seemest, Ida, like a child of air
But gone astray, and wandering pathless there
  With that aerial step, those sunny eyes
Seeking some bright seraphic messenger
  To waft thee gently to thy kindred skies,
    Thy beautiful, long remembered, long lost Paradise.

VII

And she had wandered from her own dear isle,
  The happy cradle of her innocent hours,
Where life seemed bliss, and Nature was a smile
  Though soft the shade of her beloved bowers.
And fair the Harem of her bright-eyed flowers
  That woo the amorous Sun's refulgent ray ;
Yet 'twas more sweet to watch the cloud that lowers
  Big, dark, and fateful on Eumonia's day
    Than revel in those fields, so lovely and so gay.

G

VIII

A rainbow on a stormy Heaven, she came
    To speak of happier hours, and brighter skies ;
Breathe words of love, unlike, and yet the same,
    And kiss the tears from her Eumonia's eyes,
Bidding Hope's sunshine transiently to rise.
    Then with a softly beaming smile recall
Home's dear delights, where Memory fondly flies
    The wreathed roses, and her Father's Hall,
    Where erst she gaily bloomed the fairest flower of
        all.

IX

And Ida from the bark, impetuous, flew
    Till a delightful glimpse her quick eye caught,
Sleeping on earth beneath the falling dew,
    Of the loved one her heart so fondly sought.
But oh ! Eumonia, had it ever thought
    To see thee thus, would it have throbbed and
        leapt
To meet thy smile ?   Yes ! for to share thy lot
    Is joy.   And Ida watched her as she slept,
    And gazed, and gazing turned away.   Perchance
        she wept.

LEILA : A TALE

CANTO I

He faded, and so calm and meek,
So softly worn, so sweetly weak,
So tearless, yet so tender, kind,
And grieved for those he left behind.

BYRON,

I

SWEETEST of hours! when o'er the murmuring
    seas
The fairy Elves on moonlight pillows sleep,
Or hold communion with the silent breeze,
That mutely o'er the heaving waves may creep.
Sweetest of hours! The minstrel's fingers sweep
His harp more softly when thou lingerest
Beside him, for 'tis sweet with thee to weep
Friends loved and lost, and faithless tho' caressed,
Or murmur in thine ear the name his heart loves
    best.

G 2

II

Sweetest of hours ! Thou soft and balmy shroud
To sleeping nations and the billowy sea.
Time wraps his pinions in a fleecy cloud,
And treads more lightly as he looks on thee.
Thou art the Cradle of young memory,
And Fancy doth, thy little nursling, play
Around thee, laughing at his own wild glee.
Sweetest of hours ! beneath thy gentle sway,
Tears fall more soothingly, and smiles appear more
       gay.

III

Now, 'neath the influence of thy holy star,
Tuning his trancing notes to Lady fair,
The Spanish Lover wakes the sweet guitar,
Wreathing mild music with the moonlight air.
And Venice, loveliest in her despair,
Her pristine splendour may a while forget—
Floating upon her midnight waters—where
In sportive play the lights and shades have met,
While glides thro' silvery tides the musical Gondolet.

IV

But sweeter yet the Ægean muse appears
Within the still and silent scene to sleep,
While Dian seems to smile on it thro' tears,
As on a slumbr'ing infant sighing creep
The Summer winds upon the rippling deep,
Seeming, as here they steal, more musical.
Hark ! do the Fays their nightly vigils keep,
Bearing sweet music from their airy Hall,
To catch, on moontipt wings, the shadows as they
      fall ?

V

Is it the choral shell of Ocean's Daughters,
Whose tunes invade the purity of night ?
Is it a Peri wailing from the waters,
And sighing for some visitant of light
To come and swathe her with his presence bright ?
Ah, no ! the notes that softly thus beguile
Move gaily, till the voice of laughter quite
Overwhelms their sounds—and, see, Heaven's
      starry smile
Gleams on those torch-lit towers that crown the
      Corsair's isle !

VI

Thy festive dances, Leila, thou delayest
But little, since thy father's bark hath sought
The perilous deep. Thy Maidens' smiles are
    gayest,
Thine own are brightest since the frown that
    taught
Those[1] truant, laughing eyes to mimic thought,
And that young brow to doff its playful guise,
And wear the pride a Corsair's Daughter's ought,
Hath passed away—while swift o'er Ocean flies
The Corsair's daring Bark beneath contending skies.

VII

And Otho oft had left his lovely child,
To carry terror to some distant shore,
And dare his desp'rate fortunes—for he smiled
At danger, death, and all the ills of war—
His ear found music in the cannon's roar ;
Yet when around his Leila's neck he flung
His arms, and sighed ' perhaps we meet no more,'
With quiv'ring lip he kissed her eyes' soft blue,
And breathed with falt'ring tongue a Father's fond
    Adieu.

[1] The MS. (kindly verified by Mr. Wise) has ' Thou,' with
a full stop at the end of the preceding line ; but it does not
seem possible to obtain sense from such a text.

VIII

She was his all, his happiness, his life,
The gentle spring of every soothing bliss ;
The younger image of a sainted wife,
The playful spy on each unuttered wish,
The tie that bound him to a world like this.
And oft he strove to bid her bosom rise
'Bove Youth's light smiles, and follies womanish,
To store her mind with warlike histories,
And read his glorious meed in Leila's sunny eyes !

IX

When yet a child upon her artless ear
He breathed strange tales of blood and treachery,
And if the twice told feats she seemed to hear
With infantine impatience, in his eye
Sate the deep gloom that passed not quickly by.
While panting for her sports of childish glee,
With innocent boldness, and endearments sly,
The little Captive struggled from his knee,
And clapped her infant hands, and smiled that she
        was free !

X

But now when Leila's eye of varying light
Had softened into woman's downcast gaze,
No more she swiftly sped her sportive flight
From Otho's call, but stayed a while to praise
The tongue of fame that deeds like his repays.
Then hung so tenderly on his caress,
That thou oft heard him (thus the old man says)
Even her half smothered laugh with fondness bless,
The gay, light-hearted, burst of childish happiness.

XI

Thus passed young Leila's days, and Pleasure
        seemed
The hours to colour with his rosy wing,
For so her gentle heart enchanted dreamed,
But in her father's absence she could sing
More blithely with her maids, more lightly spring
In the swift dance, enjoying every wish.
And yet, when storms on creaking pinions bring
Sea-racking winds, she longed for Otho's kiss,
And whispered ' Without *him* it cannot all be bliss.'

XII

And Otho's bark had passed the billowy seas,
And mirth and laughter rung in Otho's Hall,
Mingling their peals with the melodious breeze.
Upon the still and moonlight waters fall
The lights that blaze within that lofty wall,
Where soft-toned lutes and youthful voices meet
With Minstrel harps, the gayest notes of all,
Till music swells so murmuringly sweet
It seems the echoing sound of their light glancing
      feet !

XIII

Fair Leila leads the dance, and graceful wind
The lovely dancers, innocently gay.
With sunny brows, and hearts that leave behind
All cares, Joy wafts on painted wings away.
And smiles, in sportive mood, delighted play
From eyes to lips, from lip to glowing cheek.
But the harps cease ! confused the dancers stray,
Led slyly wrong by some wild maiden's freak,
Who laughs the gay excuse her light heart cannot
      speak.

XIV

And breathless Leila sank upon a couch,
And from her radiant, animated brow
Shook the fair ringlets—' Oh ! ' she cried, ' how
    much
I thirst for sherbet, in its maze of snow.
We dance no more to-night, at least not now—
So Zoe ! Florida ! Maidens ! sit ye down—
And, slaves, Sherbet !   No tarrying I allow !
Quick, the full bowl with sparkling lustre crown ! '
The playful Despot spake and feigned a sportive
    frown.

XV

' My Lady,' said the youthful Florida, ' sweet
Is the refreshing tide of cool sherbet,
But when soft sounds and laughing goblets meet,
Believe me, Leila, it is sweeter yet.
O for the Music I can ne'er forget,
That yesternight upon my senses fell,
As heedlessly my wandering steps I let
Glide near the Northern Turret's grated cell !
And still my wrapt soul hears that music's exquisite
    swell.'

XVI

' Who in the Northern Turret lingers, Thor ? '
Exclaimed, with eager voice, the listening maid.
' Two Captives harried from the Grecian shore,
And one a minstrel youth,' the old man said,
' For want of ransom in the dungeon laid.'
' Go ! bring him hither, I will hear him sing,
To-night, this hour, it shall not be delayed,
For my soul hangs on expectation's wings,
To hear the musical sound of that young Minstrel's
      string.'

XVII

So spake, with voice impatient, Otho's Child ;
And, springing from her couch impetuous, so
Entreatingly upon the old man smiled
That his heart melted in an honest glow
Of kind, indulgent tenderness, and tho'
Stern Otho's mandates should his steps prevent,
He only shook his silv'ry locks of snow
With smile that half reproach half kindness meant,
Gazed on her laughing brow, and blessed her as he
      went.

XVIII

O ! youth is like a year of circling springs !
Or a sweet Faeryland of trancing dreams,
Where rainbow joys and bright imaginings
On the warm landscape come in sunny gleams,
Till the young, innocent heart enchanted deems
That life is imaged by a sunny day—
And gazing with delight upon the beams
Of pleasure's wings, so rosy and so gay,
Forgets they are the plumes with which he flies away.

XIX

And, breathless with impatience, Leila stood
With hands fast clasped, and balmy lips apart,
To hear returning steps.   The eloquent blood
Rushed to her temples from her beating heart,
As wide the portal flew with echoing start.
Who comes ?   'Tis Thor, and at his side he brings
The Minstrel Boy, tho' not with step alert,
But slowly sad, unlike Youth's bounding springs,
While on his arm he bears his lute with many strings.

XX

He was a simple youth with pensive brow,
That a sad, heartrending tale might speak
Of patient suffering and enduring woe.
The pallid wanness of his sunken cheek,
And his frail form, so tremulously weak,
Told mutely health's decay and hope's alloy.
In his soft eye there dwelt a spirit meek,
And gentle, and resigned, tho' strange to joy,
For smiles indeed were strange to that poor Minstrel
     Boy.

XXI

And kindly Leila on his pale brow gazed,
Then some encouraging words of kindness spoke,
And the famed music of his young voice praised.
The Minstrel smiled not, spake not, but his look
Was grateful, as his little lute he took
Within his wasted hand, and tried to sweep
His fingers o'er it.   But the tunes awoke
Something within him that had seemed to sleep—
The hand convulsive paused, the Minstrel turned to
     weep.

XXII

'Twas but a struggle, soon and quickly o'er,
And once again his spirit calmer grew ;
And calm his saint-like forehead as before—
And if a feverish glow of warmer hue
Flushed the pale cheek, or if the eye of blue
Still glistened with a tear subdued and meek,
They were the only signs, so simply true,
That seemed, with sad expressiveness, to speak
How deep Affliction struck, how soon his heart must
      break !

XXIII

' Poor Minstrel ! ' said young Leila, and she took
One tremulous hand within her fingers fair.
It was too much, his frame convulsive shook,
And, fainting, to a couch the maidens bear
The dying youth.   He had endured despair,
Jail, hunger, anguish, slav'ry, suff'ring, pain—
But when the voice of kindness on his ear
Fell gently sweet, he sank beneath the strain,
His lone and broken heart ne'er deemed to hear again.

XXIV

'Dear Lady,' said the Minstrel's falt'ring tongue,
' Compassion's tears within those soft eyes swell,
And thy fast-beating heart is yet too young
To hear unmoved the story I might tell.
When Death forbids my flitting soul to dwell,
Heav'n is before me, but with one annoy ;
A Father lingers in a grated cell. '
' Nay ! nay ! ' said Leila, ' he shall taste the joy
Of Freedom's light ere morn—but live poor, suff'ring
    Boy ! '

XXV

' Thanks, gentle Lady, he has loved me less
Perchance than sires who play a fonder part,
Yet will he soften into tenderness
When this sad tiding shall thy slaves impart ;
For well I know he has a gentle heart,
Though sternly wedded to an idle need.
But tell him, Lady, kindest as thou art,
What calmness in my eyes he now might read,
And how his dying boy found happiness indeed.

XXVI

' Tell him, oh ! tell him of my peaceful death.
I looked for pain and found a Father's smile ;
I looked for terror's gale, and lo ! the breath
Of Paradise, to comfort and beguile.
Hope came instead of bitterness, the while
Mercy hung near on her redeeming wing.
Tell him all this, and bid him not revile !
Then give my lute, which to his mind may bring
The once beloved hand that wandered on its string.'

XXVII

' Oh ! speak not,' Leila cried, ' so mournfully !
For Hope and Freedom lend thee comfort yet,
And happiness—Thou *must* not, *shalt* not *die*—
Joy and thy destiny at last have met.
Then wilt thou Heav'n's dear gifts refuse, and let
Despair o'erwhelm the spirit erst so mild ?
Nay, glad thy youthful heart, and care forget ;
Thou wilt not suffer long,' said Otho's Child.
' No ! ' whispered that meek boy, and clasped his
        hands, and smiled !

XXVIII

Sweet was the smile, and beautiful, and faint.
Upon his pallid brow it mildly slept,
Shedding its radiance on the passing Saint !
What hand the Minstrel's desolate lute hath swept ?
'Twas but the wind that thro' the lattice kept
Its mournful music o'er the Ocean's bed.
And wildly Leila hid her face, and wept
Above that boy—she weeps upon the dead—
The fluttering pulse was still, the Minstrel's soul
     had fled.

CANTO II

But where is the now bound prisoner, where ?
CAMPBELL.

That heart has long been changed,
Worm-like 'twas trampled, adder-like avenged.
BYRON.

I

O FREEDOM is the watch-tower of the soul,
That lights the lofty thought, the flashing eye !
True as the faithful magnet to the pole
Do noble hearts to Freedom's banner fly,
Beneath its shade to conquer or to die !
And if her smile the Patriot's soul forsake,
It sinks beneath Oppression's yoke for aye,
Lone as Eolian harps, that never wake,
Save when across their chords their own wild breezes
    break.

II

Sweet Liberty ! thou art a Spirit fair
And exquisite ; the discontented Gloom,
And red-winged War, thy stormy Parents were !
Thy birthplace was the Patriot's cold, bleak tomb ;
   Racked wert thou by the sighs that mourned his
      doom ;
And when thine eyes first opened into day,
   Smilingly bright, the gathering mists t'illume,
Thy Parents howling sank beneath their ray,
To see a thing so much more beautiful than they.

III

A moonbeam sleeping on a troubled ocean,
A rainbow floating on a darkening sky,
Thou comest forth amidst the world's commotion,
Oasis of the desert ! Liberty !
Back from thy radiant brows the long locks fly,
   While shrieks the battle, and where flames the
      sword !
So midst the din of warring clouds on high
The Spirit of the Lightning walks abroad
In his sublimity, the storm's blue-pinioned Lord !

H 2

IV

' Twas midnight.   In that castle's grated cell
The lonely Captive couched.   He did not sleep,
For thoughts within his dark eye seem to dwell
Too wild for rest, for utterance too deep.
Thro' the small grate their song the cold winds
     keep ;
He tried their chilling influence to restrain
By turning from the blasts, that nearer creep,
With a stern smile, half mockery, half pain,
The heavy iron clanked, the Captive smiled again.

V

It was a ghastly gleam, that seemed to make
The darkness of his brow more terrible ;
The lip an instant moved, as if to speak
Curses, that suit a lip so dreadful well.
But the half accents withered as they fell.
Thoughts dark and wild his bosom seem to employ,
Till steps approach the entrance of his cell ;
Then o'er his pale cheek gleamed a rugged joy—
' It is,' the Father cried, ' It is, it is my boy ! '

VI

A vision stood before him. 'Twas not he,
The gentle partner of the Captive's chain,
But an aerial form that seems to be
Like those bright shapes that sometimes cross the
    brain,
When music wraps us in her transing strain.
Yet it was living, for its soft eyes swim
In Heaven's own light, reflected back again.
And it was woman, for it looked on him,
Then pitying turned away—those eyes were growing
    dim !

VII

' Stranger,' she whispered, but her voice was
    broken,
And her tone faltered, yet in that lone word,
So faint, so low, so tremulously spoken,
Something seemed breathed that tenderness
    deserved.
A thought within the Captive's soul was stirred,
And he sprang forwards with convulsive strain,
Hand clenched, and eye distended as he heard ;
Then sank exhausted on his couch again,
And pressed his anguished head upon the cold,
    damp chain.

VIII

Awed, shrinking, trembling, the young Leila stood,
Gazing upon his anguish silently ;
Her gentle heart revolving how it should
Most kindly and most tenderly reply
To the fierce question of his burning eye.
Then with a cheek averted, sadly pale,
And tottering step, approaching him more nigh,
She showed beneath her simple, roseate veil
The Minstrel's little lute—'twas all the Minstrel's
     tale !

IX

 · And eloquently well that tale it spake,
And seemed the whole distracting truth to bring
Home to the father's heart.   It did not break,
But it swelled big, as tho' 'twere labouring
With agony too weighty to take wing. ´
Fast quivered his stern lip, as hastily
He stretched his ironed hand to touch a string.
'Twas but a *touch*, but more it seemed to be—
' Thou wert my boy's,' he cried, and tears gushed
     wild and free !

X

The Father wept upon the last, last token
Of the dead child who could no longer bless.
And Leila with a voice gentle, but broken,
Gave the last words of simple tenderness
She heard his boy's beloved lips express.
She told him how he loved him, and how mild
He looked with unrepining gentleness
To Heaven, and felt his innocent soul beguiled
When Death came softly down, and freed him as he
        smiled !

XI

O Musical are the light, gay sounds that fall
From woman's lips, when joy those lips impart !
Yet softest, dearest, loveliest of all
Are her mild soothings of the aching heart,
For kindness is her most delightful Art.
And it is sweet when in the bosom lies
The throe of anguish, and afflictions smart,
To learn submission to the ruling skies,
And gather healing bliss from woman's gentle eyes.

XII

And as the trembling girl with accents soft
Spoke of his Boy, the Father mutely there
Hung on the story, never heard too oft,
And wept less wildly. Then from his despair
For the first time looked up and gazed on her,
That young bright thing that in the moonlight
    stands
So wondrous pitying, yet so very fair ;
Breathing, with swimming eyes and fast clasped
    hands,
Words sweet as summer waves rippling on yellow
    sands.

XIII

Kindly he looked upon her, with a gaze
That seemed more calm, tho' Anguish quivered
    thro' ;
And tried his hollow, tremulous voice to raise
In tones that came half smothered, hoarse, and
    low—
' Fair Being, say,' he murmured, ' Who art thou
That comest thus, the Captive's sorrow wild
To soothe with that compassionate voice and
    brow ? '
And Leila bent her head, and answered mild—
' My Father's name thou knowest, I am Otho's Child.'

XIV

Uprose the Captive in his frenzy, flashed
His raging eye in bloodshot agony ;
And with the Maniac's furious strength he dashed
The fetters wildly from him, and stood free.
' Whom made thy Father childless ? was it *me* ?
Yet, maiden, fear not, innocence will save
Even Otho's child from Death ; enough 'twill be
To render blood for blood, and grave for grave ! '
' Yet,' said the shuddering girl, ' *he* died, and *he*
    forgave.'

XV

' What, my poor boy ? Ah yes ! it was his guilt,
His gentleness, the lesson of his creed,
His madness or his weakness, what thou wilt,
To pray for his Destroyer, nor to heed
The sting that bade his innocent bosom bleed,
Save by the whispered words that sometimes spoke
His pale lips in their meekness—for indeed
My boy's heart did not coil beneath the stroke
To curse the striker—No ! it lay still, and it broke !

XVI

The Father paused, and from his tortured brow
Wiped the cold sweat that stood profusely there,
And breathed a short convulsive groan of woe.
Then in the hoarse, wild accents of despair
He hurried on—' Girl ! Otho set the snare
For the young dove defenceless and oppressed,
But he has stumbled on the tiger's lair ;
He aimed his arrow at the wild deer's breast,
But thrust his crushing heel within the adder's nest.'

XVII

' Yes ! we shall meet, the wronger and the wronged,
The Corsair and the Captive, we shall meet !
And tho' his Pirate bands around be thronged,
Yet will I rush upon him ; 'twill be sweet
To stamp his heart's blood out beneath my feet !
O musical and rapturous the clang
Of his bright arms when dust and armour greet !
But sweeter yet to watch his dying pang ! '
Grimly the Captive smiled, and loud the night winds
        sang.

XVIII

Breathless and pale the shuddering Leila lent
Her fainting form against that prison wall,
With eyes upon the raging Maniac bent,
That seemed to drink the passionate words that
    fall
(The wringings of Despair's embittered gall)
From his wild lips, and tho' her heart grew chill
And sick with dread, yet when her thoughts recall
His sufferings and his anguish, grown more bold,
These were the hurried words her trembling accents
    told.

XIX

' Ye must not, shall not meet ! for I will ope
These portals, and the smile of liberty
Shall give thee back again to life and hope.
And when, stern man, thou shalt again be free,
Should'st thou then think in some dull hour of me,
Let not revenge within thy bosom wake !
But kindly in thy memory bear that she,
Leila, the Corsair's Child, thy bonds did break ;
And O ! forgive his deeds, for his poor Daughter's
    sake ! '

XX

'Follow me quick! the small boat waits before
These towers, and Ocean ripples at its side,
Eager to waft thee to thy native shore.
Then haste! for fair the hour and fresh the tide!
My Father's frown? Ah no, he will not chide,
For often has this hand his captives freed,
And then forgiveness never was denied ;
For he's all tenderness—indeed—indeed!
And kind her Father's smile when Leila's accents
        plead.'

XXI

There was a simple pathos in the tone
Of these light words, so guileless and so few,
That sank into the heart.   And gently shone
A tear upon her cheek ; a half smile too,
As eagerly her delicate hands undrew
The iron bolts.   The spacious corridor
They pass with rapid footsteps, hurrying thro'—
Who in the moonlight stands, with dreadful lower ?
O Heaven! has Otho's bark already reached the
        shore ?

XXII

No sound or shriek did Leila's lips breathe out,
But wildly to a column's base she clung ;
For in her dizzy ear the maniac shout
Of the freed Captive like a fiend's yell rung.
And on her sight the dagger's bright blade flung
Its flickering lightning, ominous and chill.
Chief has met Chief, and foe on foe has sprung.
The grappling strain—the curse that thirsts to kill—
A pause—a rushing sound—one groan—and all was
      still !

XXIII

An instant, and the Daughter's arms were thrown
Round her fall'n Sire, while tearless agony
From her scared heart, so young and yet so lone,
Burst forth in one long, wild, convulsive cry !
A savage shout the Murderer's lips reply,
As 'neath his bloody grasp the casements crash ;
And down he leaps, with laugh of mockery,
Into the deep. The billows heavily splash,
And far before his arm the circling waters flash.

XXIV

He fled, and unobserved, tho' numerous throng
The Maidens that in Leila's love were knit,
And Chiefs that to her father's ranks belong.
To mark that scene the torch's red glare lit
Faces, where different passions darkly flit.
Horror and vengeance, curse and sympathy
Were there, in characters of terror writ.
The   breath   supprest—the   muttered   whisper's
      sigh—
The question's hurried tone that waited not reply !

XXV

' Why crowd ye round me,' said young Leila, ' so ?
I tell ye he is dead, I killed him there ! '
And a smile came across her cold, white brow,
Like moonlight on a marble sepulchre.
While, with the sickening calmness of despair,
She laid her maddened cheek close, close to his,
Twining her fingers in his bloody hair,
And pressing on his lips the same fond kiss
She gave him in her hours of happiness and bliss.

XXVI

Gently they bore her from that scene of dread,
And strove to sooth her soul, too wildly gay,
She seemed to list, but heard not what they said,
For still her wandering lips distracted say
' He died—I murdered him.' Thus, day by day,
She sank into the grave—'till one fair night,
Raising her dying eyes to Heaven to pray,
She was consoled ; then breathed, with brow of
     light,
' Dear Hinda, death is sweet—the Minstrel told us
     right.'

XXVII

'Twas the last sound her gentle accents spoke ;
And all the Poet's humble page records
Of her, whose young and filial heart was broke
By its own tenderness, are these few words.
And as the music of the sighing chords,
That weave her lone dirge with the passing gale,
This little story of her grief affords.
O ! let its influence o'er thine heart prevail,
And lend a pitying tear to Leila's simple tale !

A TRUE DREAM

(Dreamed at Sidmouth, 1833)

I HAD not an evil end in view,
  Tho' I trod the evil way ;
And why I practised the magic art,
  My dream it did not say.

I unsealed the vial mystical,
  I outpoured the liquid thing,
And while the smoke came wreathing out,
  I stood unshuddering.

The smoke came wreathing, wreathing out,
  All mute, and dark, and slow,
Till its cloud was stained with a fleshly hue,
  And a fleshly form 'gan show.

Then paused the smoke—the fleshly form
  Looked steadfast in mine ee,
His beard was black as a thundercloud,
  But I trembled not to see.

I unsealed the vial mystical,
  I outpoured the liquid thing,
And while the smoke came wreathing out,
  I stood unshuddering.

The smoke came wreathing, wreathing out,
  All mute, and dark and slow,
Till its cloud was stained with a fleshly hue,
  And a fleshly form 'gan show.

Then paused the smoke—but the mortal form
  A garment swart did veil,
I looked on it with fixed heart,
  Yea—not a pulse did fail !

I unsealed the vial mystical,
  I outpoured the liquid thing,
And while the smoke came wreathing out,
  I stood unshuddering.

The smoke came wreathing, wreathing out,
  And now it was faster and lighter,
And it bore on its folds the rainbow's hues,
  Heaven could not show them brighter.

I

Then paused the smoke, the rainbow's hues
    Did a childish face express—
The rose in the cheek, the blue in the eyne,
    The yellow in the tress.

The fair young child shook back her hair,
    And round me her arms did wreathe,
Her lips were hard and cold as stone,
    They sucked away my breath.

I cast her off as she clung to me,
    With hate and shuddering ;
I brake the vials, and foresware
    The cursed, cursed thing.

Anon outspake a brother of mine—
    ' Upon the pavement, see,
Besprent with noisome poison slime,
    Those twining serpents three.'

Anon outspake my wildered heart
    As I saw the serpent train—
' I have called up three existences
    I cannot quench again.

' Alas ! with unholy company,
　My lifetime they will scathe ;
They will hiss in the storm, and on sunny days
　Will gleam and thwart my path.'

Outspake that pitying brother of mine—
　' Now nay, my sister, nay,
I will pour on them oil of vitriol,
　And burn their lives away.'

' Now nay, my brother, torture not,
　Now hold thine hand, and spare.'
He poured on them oil of vitriol,
　And did not heed my prayer.

I saw the drops of torture fall ;
　I heard the shriekings rise,
While the serpents writhed in agony
　Beneath my dreaming eyes.

And while they shrieked, and while they writhed,
　And inward and outward wound,
They waxed larger, and their wail
　Assumed a human sound.

And glared their eyes, and their slimy scales
　　Were roundly and redly bright,
Most like the lidless sun, what time
　　Thro' the mist he meets your sight.

And larger and larger they waxed still,
　　And longer still and longer ;
And they shrieked in their pain, ' Come, come to us,
　　We are stronger, we are stronger.'

Upon the ground I laid mine head,
　　And heard the wailing sound ;
I did not wail, I did not writhe—
　　I laid me on the ground.

And larger and larger they waxed still
　　And longer still and longer ;
And they shrieked in their pangs, ' Come, come to us,
　　We are stronger, we are stronger.'

Then up I raised my burning brow,
　　My quiv'ring arms on high ;
I spake in prayer, and I named aloud
　　The name of sanctity.

And as in my anguish I prayed and named
  Aloud the holy name,
The impious mocking serpent voice
  Did echo back the same.

And larger and larger they waxed still,
  And stronger still and longer !
And they shrieked in their pangs, ' Come, come to us,
  We are stronger, we are stronger.'

Then out from among them arose a form
  In shroud of death indued—
I fled from him with wings of wind,
  With whirlwinds he pursued.

* * * *

I stood by a chamber door, and thought
  Within its gloom to hide ;
I locked the door, and the while forgot
  That I stood on the outer side.

And the knell of mine heart was wildly tolled
  While I grasped still the key ;
For I felt beside me the icy breath,
  And knew that *that* was *he*.

I heard these words, ' Whoe'er doth *taste*,
   Will *drink* the magic bowl ;
So her body may do my mission here
   Companioned by her soul.'

Mine hand was cold as the key it held,
   Mine heart had an iron weight ;
I saw a gleam, I heard a sound—
   The clock was striking eight.

EPISTLE TO A CANARY

THE manuscript of the ensuing ' Epistle to a Canary '
has not hitherto been printed, or even described.
The verses, in the handwriting of the author, were
preserved among the Browning MSS. until their dispersal after Robert Barrett Browning's death.   The
' Epistle ' bears no title, place, or date, but it is not
difficult to reconstruct its history with some exactness.
There can be no doubt that it was addressed to Mary
Russell Mitford's pet canary, from 74 Gloucester
Place, Portman Square, the Barretts' London house
since 1835.   The acquaintance of Miss Barrett with
Miss Mitford began in May 1836.   Formal at first,
in a few months it ripened into a close and tender
intimacy.   Late in January 1837 the country friend
paid a visit, apparently her first, to 74 Gloucester
Place, and saw the various pets, and the ways of
the Barrett family, a knowledge of which seems pre-
supposed in the ' Epistle.'   It was about this time

that Elizabeth wrote her poem, ' The Doves,' which
was published in *The Seraphim* of 1838, beginning

> My little doves have left a nest
> Upon an Indian tree.

It is one of this pair of doves who is supposed to
indite the epistle to Miss Mitford's canary. Both
ladies expatiated in their correspondence on the merits
of their ' dear pets,' and letters exist in which they
have sentimentally exchanged canary-feathers. Miss
Mitford boasted herself a ' complete bird-fancier.' I
think it possible that the present ' Epistle ' may be
connected with that ' story of the Doves ' which
Mary Russell Mitford acknowledges in a letter of
February 22, 1837. At all events the ' Epistle '
must be earlier in date than August 16, 1837, when
Elizabeth Barrett announced that ' a new little dove
had appeared from a shell, over which nobody had
prognosticated good.' It is incredible that, if so
thrilling an occurrence had already taken place when
the ' Epistle ' was written, no mention should be made
of it by the enthusiastic parent.

The poem is one of many loose and pleasant private
missives in verse which Miss Barrett indulged in
during those early years. It is valuable from the
information it gives about the household at Gloucester

Place, the birds, the dog Myrtle, William the butler,
the shrouded and limited existence of the poet, with
its windows wide open to the horizons of the
imagination.—EDMUND GOSSE.

DEAR unknown friend, esteemed Canary !
I've read your letter sent by Mary.
I've read it with sufficient pleasure
To draw a joyous choral measure
From all the birds in Vallombrosa,—
A place you've heard of, I suppose, Sir.

My spouse and I accept the honor
You put upon me and upon her,
And here with equal cordiality
Return our friendship's mutuality.
It is indeed a high communion,
When hearts of birds can meet in union,
And mine beneath my wing is beating,
Just like a lark's, the sunshine greeting,
To think that I, whose sun's a masked one,
Have still your friendship to be basked in ;
That I and my companion, fated
To be for aye expatriated,
To sit at London windows, viewing,
For fair green hills, the human ruin,

Hearing, for river-songs, wind-catches,—
' Old clothes, old clothes,' and ' Buy my matches,'—
Should still have friendship's sweet assistance
From songful spirits at a distance.
For here is human friendship only,
And Mrs. Dove and I are lonely ;
And tho' on seasons out of number,
We're kissed by human lips to slumber ;
And tho' we feel caresses loving
Drawn round our eyelids, without moving—
And nestle upon hands, confiding,
As if in forest-shadows hiding ;
And even condescend to show us
Obedient when some tongues speak to us ;
Yet, after all, this human love,
Dear Sir, what is it to a Dove ?
It is not quite as cruel, truly,
As I did think, (I own, unduly,)
When first the dreadful reasoning creature
Surprised me in the hush of nature ;
But still 'tis poor and sad, half folly,
Half wildness, and whole melancholy ;
And if we were not near each other,
We should have only you, my brother,
To keep our spirits from dejection,
While darkened so with man's affection.

And now dear brother-friend, Canary,
It seemeth to me necessary
To write a portrait of the being
You deign to value without seeing ;
That, having read it, inartistic
As it may be, and egoistic,
You may attain a clearer notion
Of one who loves you to devotion.

My feathers,—do not think me proud,—
Are colored faintly as a cloud,
A fair brown cloud at dawn of day,
Which bears, within a golden ray,
A secret kept, which all the way
Shines out for joy. My feet are red,
Contrastingly, as used to tread
Bright sunset clouds, and thence retaining
The colour of their crimson staining ;
My golden eyes may each have drawn
A spark of light from highest dawn,
Which glows and opens, as you view them,
Till sunset reds are likest to them ;
Nor marvel that I so have won mine
Image out of clouds and sunshine,
When ancestors of mine, above them,
So often flew as Venus drove them,

And on my neck I still am wearing
The yoke-mark, which their part was, bearing
A fair light mark, my neck enringing,
A rainbow out of darkness springing ;
I would not change it for your singing ;
Tho' certainly Anacreon's story
Detracts a little from the glory,
Saying she sold him ' for a song ' our
Grandsire, most insulting wronger ;
But some, in dear esteem who hold us,
Declare she never would have sold us,—
Not for an epic, whose aroma
Was all of amarynths and Homer.

Enough ! No peacock's tail, a glowing
Upon earth's darkest dust bestowing,
Is swept by me (*my* tail partaketh
The universal shade she maketh !) ;
And yet with such a graceful motion
I rise and stoop like waves on ocean,
I hear applied what one expresses
. About ' majestic lowlinesses.'
A sudden fear, reflection raises,—
' What will he think of these self-praises ? '
But, dear king friend, we birds inherit
No mounting and immortal spirit ;

Our souls are our fair forms, and we do
More glory in them than men need do.
Yet beauty is not all, nor doubt me
(In naming other things about me),
I am too modest e'er to quarrel
With such as you for music's laurel,—
I mean for science! All my chanting
Was learnt from winds and waves descanting ;
A solemn sweetness is its feature,
A sad slow monotone of nature,—
The fall of dew and leaf resembling
So much, it sets my bosom trembling
With a soft memory-passion, mourning
For things to which is no returning.
Alas ! Alas ! what am I doing ?
I break into a sudden cooing—
Forgive me ! tho' myself affected,
I would not make my friend dejected.
And seriously considered, cages,
Tho' portions of the iron ages,
Are not, for all their wires, to shut us
From many true delights that suit us.
For all their iron wires, they loose us
To our ' adversity's sweet uses ' ;
And I myself am quite aware of
A deepened inward sense, a care of

More intellectual things, than found me
With only woods and skies around me.
For instance, what imagination
Of bird, at large in the creation,
Tho' wont in flights sublime to risk it,
E'er reached a vision of white biscuit ?

To balance this, I own at present
Some circumstances are unpleasant,
And the associates I am able
To mix with, are exceptionable ;
There is a little dog whose name is
Myrtle ! Oh, that aught so famous
To doves and Venus as that tree is
Should lend its name to such as he is !
But so it is, and, speaking justly,
This Myrtle's neither fierce nor crusty,
A poor dull worthy dog, reposing
All day beside the fire, with nose in
The rug, and eyes half shut, which show them
Properly meek, whene'er we do them
The honor of approaching to them.
Yet this same Myrtle (will you credit
The monstrous statement when you've read it ?)
With insolent affrontery, hath in
The water placed for us to bathe in

Immersed his nose, and fall'n to drinking,
As if a common fountain-brink on ;
And this offence has been repeated
Twice, thrice or four times, and we meet it
With proper indignation, springing
Towards him with a martial singing
In our wings, and fiercely wave them
About his head, who dares not brave them,
But walks away, retiring slowly,
To show he is not servile wholly !
A worthy dog, in his totality,—
Tho' wanting tact and ideality.

Then there's a parrot with its staring
Black eyes, and insolence past bearing,
Our own compatriot, (Cain was Abel's,
As heard our grand-dame 'mong the cables
Of Noah's ark,) and green, most vernally
As if our tropic woods eternally
Had stained his wings, without bestowing
The calmness *their* deep heart is knowing ;
For *she* is full of stir and meanness,
More anxious after *blue* than greenness ;
Her native screechings trans-atlantic,
Commingling with a slang pedantic

Of ' what's a clock ? ' (Degenerate folly,
A bird take note of time ! !) or ' Polly
Put on the kettle ' or ' Water Cresses ' ! !
I name with horror these excesses,
And feel, from inward indignation,
I would not stoop t' articulation
Not even of Greek,—tho' tempted sorest,—
Not for a green nest in a forest !
This parrot habits, as is proper,
A lower room, and we, an upper,
And neither of us often views her
Except when people introduce her,
And then, dear friend, you'd really wonder
To see how she would keep us under,—
As if, besides her linguist powers, her
Tail was twice as long as ours are !
Devouring all our seed, or wasting—
Objecting even to our tasting.
Of course we would resist but (praise me !)
High-tree-born birds have delicacy—
And then—and then—if I must speak, Sir,
She has, besides her eyes, a beak, Sir !
My own compatriot with such candour
Being portrayed, acquit of slander
My true opinion of another,
Whose honor 'twas, to call you brother ;

Canary was he, even as you are,
Tho' his accomplishments were fewer.
A pretty sprightly bird, that never
Reflected, hopping on for ever
With more of volatile giration
Than could deserve my admiration,
My spouse, myself, and Myrtle, eyeing
By turns, and sometimes even prying
Into my nest,—which was most trying,—
Was! is not.   He is gone! one morning,
He flew whence there is no returning
Beyond the opened panes,—to hie him
Where human kind could not come nigh him.
Well! peace be his! may he have rested,
Where every bird is music-breasted,
Where shines the sun on Ax or Yarrow,
United to some gentle sparrow.

And now, dear friend, I must pursue mine
Account, by noticing the human.
May you the generous fates have brought, where
Are none who don long coats and short hair,
But if, of those dread beings, any
Are near you, near to me are many ;
And we may speak of griefs resembling,
In friendship's sympathetic trembling.

K

Alas! dear friend! what awful noises
They make with footsteps and with voices!
With what a clashing laugh they tease us!
How roughly by our tails they seize us!
And, in our sweetest chantings, cry out
(Have they *no* ear for music?) ' Quiet!!'
There's one,—I think they call him William,—
A hawk's or vulture's soul must fill him!
For every day he's sternly able
To lay a red cloth on the table
And then a white one, like the lightning
Flashing wide! It is *too* frightening!
Our very senses seem retreating,
And really,—we can't go on eating.

You'll wish that he would come this minute,
To end a scrawl with so much in it,
And so, farewell! You will not wonder
That metre-rules I've written under;
Creation's self's a poem, written
In lovelier rhymes than I have hit on;
And I was taught by winds pathetic,
Thro' shaken woods, to be poetic.
Besides I sit,—perhaps you know it?—
Close to a human feeble poet;
And tho' her verse is very wanting

In all that beautifies my chanting
Yet still she learns in nature's college,
And has a little sound dove-knowledge ;
And I confess,—now don't discover
I condescend too much,—I love her !
At least you'll pardon me, Canary !
You love a human thing like Mary !

Farewell ! we are not of one feather,
Yet surely would agree together,
And, tho' apart, believe the love
You're held in by

        your faithful

            DOVE.

PS.
I'm very glad you've heard of Bella.
You'd hear but good, were *I* the teller !
Had I an eagle's sky-dominion,
I still would let her stroke my pinion.

THE MAIDEN'S DEATH

[This poem is one of a number of early poems by
Elizabeth Barrett Barrett, as she then was, which are
contained in a quarto MS. volume disposed of at the
sale of Browning MSS. in 1913. ' The Maiden's Death '
is undated, but stands among others, one of which bears
the date 1839. It was first printed in the *Cornhill
Magazine*, December 1913.]

Is she dying ? ye who grieve
Do answer ' Yea.'   And will she leave
Our world so soon, and separate be
From this life's unresting sea, . . .
Where the harpies' ghastly motion
Hovers ; and the wind's hoarse passion
Raves ; and there's no room nor rest
For the halcyon's fabled nest ?—
From these depths the heavens draw
Her drops of life by nature's law,
To form cloud in angels' sight,
Illumined by the great god light.

She is dying, ye who know
Beauty's fairness in a show—
Youth's high dreams where angels enter,
Dreamt on some low peradventure—
Wealth's soft strewing of the ways,
Love's deep vowing in self praise—
Weep for her who doth remove
From beauty, youth, wealth—ay! and love!
But . . . but *ye*—for I am turning
Unto some of wider learning—
Ye who know how tears find place
'Twixt the show-mask and the face—
How dream-pillows slide away
Leaving foreheads on the clay—

How the foot may smoothly tread,
While the thornwreath pricks the head—
How the mouth, with love-vows laden,
Soon . . . oh, weep not for that maiden!

Dust to dust! She lies beneath
The stone which speaks to life of death!
Young, beauteous, wealthy 'neath the sun,
And loved! yet who weep for her? *None*.

TO ROBERT LYTTON

[This poetical tribute, interesting alike from its literary and its personal connection, was first printed in the *Cornhill Magazine* for May, 1914, where the editor appended the following note :—

The Editor tenders grateful thanks, on his own behalf and that of his readers, to Mrs. Barrett Browning for her generous gift to him of the original manuscript which is here printed. For more than sixty years this tribute, by the authoress of ' Aurora Leigh,' to Robert Lytton (Edward Robert Bulwer-Lytton, 2nd Baron and 1st Earl Lytton, 1831–91), more generally known as ' Owen Meredith,' has been forgotten.

The poem was written at Bagni di Lucca in the summer of 1853, when Robert Lytton, then an attaché at the Florence Legation, was staying with the Brownings. It was here too, when he was with them again in 1857, that he had a severe attack of gastric fever and was nursed by Robert Browning. Robert Lytton had scarcely recovered when ' Penini ' Browning, a boy of eight years, was similarly attacked, but in a mild form ; during his illness, seeing his mother's anxious face bending over him, the child said, ' Think it's a little boy in the street ; and you won't feel so badly.'

The MS. is in the clear but delicate caligraphy of Mrs. Browning, without a single correction, and written on both sides of a half-sheet of paper, with a deep gash in the upper edge. The MS. was formerly in the

possession of Miss Browning, who copied on a large sheet
the full text of the three stanzas imperfect in the torn
original. Miss Browning gave both of these MSS.
to Mrs. Barrett Browning, who has kept them until
to-day ' in a little box of personal treasures.']

I

O NOBLE heart, noble soul, live
  Our leader, and king of us all !
Take the love which we languish to give ;
  Give the love without which we must fall.

II

You—brave shoulders of Atlas, just strong enough
  To bear up a world much in want of it !
You—the wise heart that's probed our life long
    enough
  To pardon the nonsense and cant of it !

III

An eye that looks straight on to God,
  And a tongue that can baffle the Devil,—
A wit that walks forth silver-shod,
  And sets a fair front against Evil.

IV

· When you speak—as you speak—I think Paul
 At Athens, posterity teaching,
Said such words, thought such thoughts, just let fall
 Such grand language as yours, in his preaching.

·

V

Yet bear with us ! think for us ! speak for us !
 There is none we can honor above you.
When you think, our own thoughts are too weak for
  us,—
 When you speak, we are silent—and love you.

VI

You are strong : we are weak and the jostle
 Of life seems to hurt us too much :
But you, O beloved, O apostle,
 Leave healing behind in your touch.

VII

Light and warmth—the whole of you piling
 Its own magnificent gladness :
But he that would prove your wise smiling
 Must have probed all the sources of sadness

VIII

For o'er depth below depth of your being
　Unfathomed the soul of you sleeps :
And your great smile is still too all seeing,
　A rainbow that arches the deeps.

IX

All that strength ! all that power ! yet so pliant !
　You're so great we could never come near you,
Were it not that the child with the giant
　Is mixed—and we honor—not fear you.

X

O but for old times for one moment !
　How we'd hymn you and crown you, and bring you
Through the Forum with praising and comment.
　Stepping proud o'er the flowers we'd fling you.

XI

We'd die for you gladly, if need were,—
　And gladly we'd live while we might for you ;
We'd follow wherever your lead were,
　Believe in you, hope for you, fight for you.

XII

These are words, now ! and yet—Oh yet live
   Our leader and king of us all !
Take the love which is all we can give !
   Take large meanings for deeds that are small !

1853

MISS ELIZABETH BARRETT BARRETT'S CRITICISMS ON SOME OF HER FUTURE HUSBAND'S POEMS (1845)

[From a¹ MS., consisting of 56 pages, octavo, found among her papers and included in the sale of the Browning Collections, in 1913. Some extracts were published in an article ' Of the Browning MSS.' by Sir Frederic G. Kenyon, K.C.B., in the *Cornhill Magazine*, August 1913 (see page ix).]

A SOUL'S TRAGEDY

> One who don't forego—
> The after-battle work—

Strictly speaking, is not ' doesn't ' the right abbreviation for only the third person ? I don't —he doesn't. 'Who won't go' you might say with accuracy, perhaps.

' Who's me '—it sounds awkward—' what's I ? ' Yet I doubt altogether what fine part of the dialogue all this is. Would ' what's me ' sound less awkward ? ' What's me '—' it's man in me.' Yes, I think it should be ' what ' : for the relation of the ' it ' afterwards.

> Wast not enough that I must strive, I said,
> To grow so far familiar with all you
> As find and take some way to get you—which
> To do, an age seemed far too little.

There is something obscure, as it strikes me in the expression of this. 'As to find' seems necessary to the construction. But 'all you' (besides) appears to lead the thought from Eulalia, and you mean Eulalia—I think. The reader will doubt here, and have first and second thoughts.

Nor missed a cloak from wardrobe, nor a dish from table

Why such a dragging line just here? An oversight, probably. The second 'nor a' might drop out to advantage.

THE FLOWER'S NAME

But this—so surely this met her eye

Is it hypercritical to complain of the 'this eye'? I seldom like the singular 'eye'—and then, when it is a Spanish eye! The line is not a great favourite of mine altogether—and the poem *is*—and you see the least speck on a Venice glass: and if it is '*my fancy*' at least I speak it off my mind and have done with it. The beauty and melody we never shall have done with . . . none of us.

Flower, you Spaniard, look you grow not.

I inquire if it should not be 'look *that* you grow not.'

Mind the pink shut mouth opens never.

A clogged line—is it not ?   Difficult to read.

> Roses, are you so fair after all ?

And I just ask whether to put it in the affirmative
thus—

> Roses, ye are not so fair after all,

does not satisfy the ear and mind better ?   It is only
asking, you know.

SIBRANDUS SCHAFNABURGENSIS

> And under the arbutus and laurustine.

Are these pluralities quite correct ?   You know
best. . . . And I doubt, at worst.   If you wrote :

> And under the arbute and laurustine

it would seem to me a more *consistent* course . . .
but I do not attempt even to decide.

> Oh the droppings have played their tricks.

' Oh well have the droppings ' you had written—
and better written, I think.

> While slowly our poor friend's leaves were swamping,
> Clasps cracking, and covers suppling.

Or query . . . ' while clasps were cracking and
covers suppling.'   A good deal is to be said for the
abrupt expression of the ' text ' . . . but the other
is safer . . . and less trusting the reader.   You
will judge.   Do you know that this poem is a great

favourite with me—it is so new, and full of a creeping, crawling grotesque life. Ah, but . . . do you know besides, it is almost reproachable in you to hold up John Knox to derision in this way !

THE BOY AND THE ANGEL

Morning, noon, eve and night.

Do you prefer this to

Morning, evening, noon and night—
for rhythm, I mean ?

As if thy voice to-day.

I think you must have meant to write

As well as if thy voice to-day.

Not that the short lines are not good in their *places*.

In heaven God said ' nor day nor night
Brings one voice of my delight.'

Taking this verse with the context, will you consider if ' God said in heaven ' is not of a simple and rather solemner intonation. The next line I do not like much. It might be more definite in meaning I think.

Entered the empty cell
And played the craftsman well

Do you prefer to have short lines in this place, and why ?

> Then forth sprang Gabriel's wings, off fell
> The flesh, remained the cell.

Is not something wrong here ?   If you mean that the flesh remained in the cell (named before), you do not say ; and what else is said ?

> To the east with prayer he turned :
> And in the angel burned.

I like and see plainly this burning in of the angel upon Theocrite as he looks to the east ; but I doubt whether it will be as clear to all readers, you suggest it so very barely.   Would not a touch or two improve the revelation ?   Do think.

> Be again the boy all curled.

At any rate you will write ' be then again ' . . . will you not ?   But I doubt about the curled boy— any one ' *becurled* ' may be right—but a curled boy ' tout rond ' does strike me as of questionable correctness.   Think, yourself.   And I do ask you to think besides, whether a little dilation of the latter stanzas of this simple noble ballad would not increase the significance and effect of the whole.   Readers will not see at a glance all you have cast into it, unless you make more *surface*—it is my impression, at least.

THE TOMB AT ST. PRAXED'S

> Old Gandolf *came me in*, despite my care,
> For a shrewd snatch, &c.

Is that ' came me in ' a correct expression . . or, rather, does it *express*? . . . Does it not make the meaning hard to get at?

This is a wonderful poem, I think, and classes with those works of yours which show most power . . most unquestionable genius in the high sense. You force your reader to sympathise positively in his glory in being buried! And what a grand passage that is, beginning—

> And then, Lord, I shall lie through centuries
> And hear the blessed mutter of the mass, &c.

THE LABORATORY

> The soul from those strong grey eyes—say no.

Will you read this line with the context, and see if the rhythm is not perplexed in it?

Could I keep them but one half minute fixed, she'd fall.

Why not ' she would fall '?

> Not that I bid you spare her pain.

And the rhythm here ! Is it well done that it should change ?

But brush the dust off me, *lest horror then springs.*

The last words are clogged, I think . . . and the expression seems forced.

ENGLAND IN ITALY. AUTUMN AT SORRENTO

> While I lull you asleep till he's o'er
> With his black in the skies.

I don't like ' he's o'er ' much, or at all perhaps. There is something to me weak and un-sirocco-like in the two contractions. Would

> Till he carries
> His black from the skies

be more *active* ?

> 'Twas time, for your long dry autumn.

I just doubt if ' and dry ' might not improve the rhythm—doubt. Only if the emphasis is properly administered to ' long,' nothing of course is wanted —only, again, it is trusting to the reader !

> What was in store.

Surely ' what change ' or what fate ' or some

additional word should assist the rhythm in this place. The line is broken and short.

Touch the strange lamps.

I do like all this living description—living description which never lived before in poetry, and now will live always.   These fishes have suffered no earth-change, though they lie here so grotesquely plain between rhyme and rhyme.   And the grave fisher too—and the children ' brown as his shrimps ' !

You see round his neck.

Why not ' and you see round his neck ' . . . for rhythm ?   The line stops you : and you need not stop, when you are looking at him, to ' see round his neck.'

The treading of the grapes is admirable painting— that ' breathless he grows ' so true to life—and the effort to ' keep the grapes under '—all admirable.

Back to my side, etc.

Is not some word, some dissyllable (as if you were to write ' back again,' &c.) wanted for rhythm— reading it with the preceding line ?

Ever some new head and breast of them.

Should it not be written ' with ever some, etc.' ?

These mountains and their infinite movement are finely true.

> How the soft plains they look on and love so
> As they would pretend ﹐
> Tower beneath them—(lower).

I do not see the construction.   Is ' lower ' put here as a verb ? and, if correctly, is it clearly, so put.

> All's silent and grave.

Why not ' all is silent and grave,' without abbreviation ?   The rhythm gains by it, I think.

> Greenly as ever.

Would not ' *as* greenly as ever ' take the rhythm on better ?

> Years cannot sever.

Quaere : . . ' and years ' or ' For years.'

> Though the one breast high in the water

Quaere . . . ' bosom-high ' for rhythm.

> When shall we sail there together.

You have effaced . . . ' Oh when shall we.'   But the exclamation seems wanted for rhythm and expression—does it not ?

> Oh to sail round them, close over

L 2

The line is broken, I think.   Should it not either be

> And oh, to sail round them,

or

> Oh, to sail round and round them ?

> That ruffle the grey sea-water.

Why not ' The grey ocean water ' for rhythm ?   All beautiful description.

> The square black tower on the largest.

Did you write ' *built* on the largest '—because the eternal rhythm?   How tired you are !   *as you said once to me.*

> Strikes the great gloom.

For clearness, the personal pronoun is wanted, I fancy.   What ' strikes ' ?

> And now come out, you best one.

Quaere, if it would not be well to repeat the ' come out '—

> And now come out, come out, &c.

> The priests mean to stamp.   (stomp).   R.B.

But is this word ' stamp,' and is it to rhyme to ' pomp.' I object to that rhyme—*I* ! !

I think it will strike you, when you come to finish

this unfinished poem, that all the rushing and hurrying life of the descriptions of it, tossed in one upon another like the grape bunches in the early part, and not ' kept under ' by ever so much breathless effort on the poet's part, can be very little adapted to send anybody to sleep. . . even if there were no regular dinner in the middle of it all. Do consider. For giving the *sense of Italy*, it is worth a whole library of travel-books.

ITALY IN ENGLAND

A serene, noble poem this is—an heroic repose in it—but nothing to imagine queries out of, with whatever good will. I like the simplicity of the great-heartedness of it (though perhaps half Saxon in character), with the Italian scenery all round—it is very impressive.

> I would grasp Metternich until
> I felt his throat, and had my will.

After all the abjuring of queries, . . . is not ' had my will ' a little wrong ?—*I would what I would.* There is a weakness in the expression. Is there not ?

PICTOR IGNOTUS—FLORENCE

> like a thunder sunk
> To the centre of an instant.

Is there not something obscure in the expression ?
And it is all so fine here, that you should let the
reader stand up as straight as he can to look round.

> Or rapture drooped her eyes as when her brood
> Pull down the nesting dove's heart to its place.

A most exquisite image, and perfect in the
expression of it, I think.

> Ever new hearts made beat and bosoms swell.

The construction seems to be entangled a little
by this line ; and the reader pauses, he clears
meaning to himself. Why not clear it for him by
writing the line thus, for instance ?—

> New hearts being made to beat, and breasts to swell.

Or something better which will strike you. Will
you consider ?

> And thus to reach my home, where Age should greet.

Should you not write it . . . . ' Of reaching thus
my home,' &c. ? The construction taking you back

to what he dreamed of—first he dreamed ' of going,' and then ' of reaching ' his home, &c.—

And then not go to heaven, &c.

Fine, all this !

These men may buy us, sell us, &c.

Meaning pictures, by ' *us*.'   But the reader cannot see it until afterwards, and gets confused.   Is it not so ? And, moreover, I do think that by a touch or two you might give a clearer effect to the previous verses about the ' gibing,' &c.   This poem is so fine, so full of power, as to claim every possible attention to the working of it ; it begins greatly, grandly, and ends so—the winding up winds up the soul in it. The versification, too, is noble—and altogether it classes with your finest poems of the length. Does it not in your own mind ? I cannot tell you how much it impresses mine.

THE CONFESSIONAL

With love and truth his brow was bright.

Looked bright—*seemed* so—should it not be, for the meaning ?

And lo !—there, smiled the father's face.

You know the best, of course ; but to me, it seems

strange that she should have seen ' the father's face ' at all in the shadow of that scaffold.

> No part in aught they hope or fear !
> No heaven with them, &c.

You think at first that she means to abjure having any part with them ; but afterwards the constructions seems to swing round to another side. Does not this stanza require clearing by a moment's attention ? It is a striking, thrilling poem too, to make it quite worth while.

GHENT TO AIX

You have finely distanced the rider in Rookwood here—not that I should think of saying so, if we had not talked of him before. You have the very trampling and breathing of the horses all through ; and the sentiment is here in its right place, through all the physical force and display. Then the difficult management of the *three* horses, of the *three* individualities ; and Roland carrying the interest with him triumphantly. I know you must be proud of the poem ; and nobody can forget it who has looked at it once.

Lokeren, the cocks crew and twilight seemed clear.

I doubt about ' twilight seeming clear.' Is it a happy expression ? But I only *doubt*, you know. The leaping up of the sun afterward, and the cattle standing black against him, and staring through the mist at the rider,—all that,—I do not call it *picture*, because it is so much better: it is the very sun and mist and cattle themselves.

And I like the description of Roland; I like *him*— seeing him; with one sharp ear bent back and the other pricked out—it is so livingly the horse, even to me who know nothing of horses in the ordinary way of sitting down and trying to remember what I know, but who recognise this for a real horse galloping. By the way, how the ' galloping ' is a good galloping word ! And how you felt it, and took the effect up and dilated it by repeating it over and over in your first stanza, . . . doubling, folding one upon another, the hoof-treads.

> I *galloped*, Dirck *galloped*, we *galloped* all three.
> Good speed cried the watch as the east gate undrew ;
> Good speed from the wall, to us galloping through.
> The gate shut the porter, the light sank to rest,
> And into the midnight we *galloped* abreast.

One query at the last stanza.

That they saved to have drunk our duke's health in but grieved.

You mean to say . . . ' would have grieved ' . . . do you not ? The construction seems a little imperfect.

TIME'S REVENGES

He does though ; and if some vein.

Will you consider, taking the context, whether ' he
does himself ' would not be better ?

> If I lived to try
> I should just turn round nor ope an eye.

Do you like ' nor ope an eye ' ?   I cannot much.
Nor do I like the ' living to *try*.'   You see how
I tell you the truth.   *My* truth.   As I fancy I see
the truth.

> As all my genius, all my learning
> Leave me, where there's no returning.

Is not that in the last line . . . somewhat weak
and indefinite, for *you* ?

> And purchase her the dear *invite*.

I protest zealously against that word.   Now isn't
it a vulgarism, and out of place altogether here ?
It seems to me, while I appreciate the conception of
this poem fully, and much admire some things in it,
that it requires more finishing than the other poems—
I mean particularly the first part, but may be as wrong
as possible notwithstanding.   I do beseech you in

regard to all these notes to separate the right from the wrong as carefully as possible ! And in the hope of your doing so, I have ventured to put down every thing that came into my head.

E. B. B.

SAUL

Part I

> Nor till from his tent

Would you not rather write ' until ' here, to break the course of monosyllables, with another reason ?

> For in the black midtent silence
> three drear days.

A word seems omitted before silence—and the short line is too short to the ear—not to say that ' drear days ' conspires against ' dread ways ' found afterwards. And the solemn flow of these six lines should be uninterrupted, I think.

The entrance of David into the tent is very visible and characteristic—and you see his youthfulness in the activity of it—and the repetition of the word ' foldskirts ' has an Hebraic effect.

> But soon I descried
> Something more black than the blackness.

Should it not be ' A something '?—more definitely ?
And the rhythm cries aloud for it, it seems to me.

> The vast, upright—

Quære—' *the* upright '. . . for rhythm ?

> Then a sunbeam burst thro' the blind tent-roof
> Showed Saul.

Now, will you think whether to enforce the admirable effect of your sudden sunbeam, this first line
should not be rendered more rapid by the removal
of the clogging epithet ' blind '—which you repeat,
too, I believe, farther on in the next page.   What if
you tried the line thus—

> Then a sunbeam that burst through the tent-roof—
> Showed Saul !

The manifestation in the short line appears to me
completer, from the rapidity being increased in the
long one.   I only *ask*—It is simply an impression—
I have told you how very fine I do think all this
showing of Saul by the sunbeam—and how the more
you come to see him, the finer it is.   The ' All heavily
hangs,' as applied to the king-serpent, you quite feel
in your muscles.

Part II

The breaking of the band of lilies round the harp is a relief and refreshment in itself after that dreadful sight. And then how beautifully true it is that the song should begin so . . . with the sheep—

> As one after one
> Docile they come to the pen-door.

But the rhythm should not interrupt itself where the sheep come docilely—and is not a word wanted . . . a syllable rather . . . before that ' Docile.' Will you consider ?

' The long grasses stifling the water.' How beautiful *that* is !

> One after one seeks its lodging
>   As star follows star
> Into the blue far above us,
>   —So blue and so far !

It appears to me that the two long lines require a syllable each at the beginning, to keep the procession of sheep uninterrupted. The ear expects to read every long and short line in the sequence of this metre as one long line. And where it cannot do so, a loss . . . an abruption . . . is felt—and there should be nothing abrupt in the movement of these pastoral, starry images. Do you think so ? Is it not Goethe who compares the stars to sheep ? Which you reverse here.

Part III

Would we might help thee, my brother ?

Why not ' Oh, would,' &c.—it throws a wail into the line, and swells the rhythm rightly, I think.

> Next she whom we count
> The beauty, the pride of our dwelling.

Why not ' For the beauty '—or ' As the beauty ' ?

> But I stopped—for here, in the darkness
> Saul groaned.

Very fine—and the preceding images full of beauty and characteristic life !—but in this long line, I just ask if the rhythm would gain by repeating ' here ' . . . thus—

> But I stop here—for here in the darkness—

I just ask, being doubtful.

And the shaking of the tent from the shudder of the King. . . What effect it all has !—and I like the jewels *waking* in his turban !

> So the head—but the body stirred not.

If you wrote ' So the head—but the body . . . *that* stirred not.' Just see the context.

Part IV

> The water was wont to go warbling
> Softly and well.

Is not a syllable wanted at the beginning of the short line, to make the water warble softly . . . 'right softly' ?

> And heard her faint tongue
> Join in, while it could, to the witness.

Would ' Joining in ' be better to the ear ?

> And promise and wealth for the future.

I think you meant to write ' the ' before promise.

All I said about the poem in my note, I think more and more. Full of power and beauty it is,—and the conception, very striking.

E. B. B.

LURIA

Act I, Scene 1.

> And vaunted Luria, Luria, who but he ?

Whom but *him*—is it not ?

> This Moor of the bad faith, etc.

You say afterwards ' The boy ' and ' the stranger.' Why not ' This boy ' and ' this stranger ' to carry forward the emphasis ?

> Which pass not, to yourself no question put.

You are fond of that *absolute* construction—but I think that sometimes it makes the meaning a little doubtful, and here there is some weakness from the inversion—you simply mean to say—' Which, do not pass without consideration.' Then, the '*put*' is a bad word at all times to my ear.

Who think themselves your lords, such slaves are they ?

Do you gain anything by the inversion ? If you write ' They are such slaves,' do you not on the contrary gain in force of opposition, propriety of accent, and directness ?

If as you bid this sentence they pronounce.

I cease to protest against the frequent inversions. Why not simply

If they pronounce this sentence as you bid ?

Is there an objection ? And it gives the effect, I think, of more impulse to these noble lines.

From the adoring army at his back

Query—from *that* adoring.
How I like

That thin flitting instantaneous steel
Against the blind bull front of a brute-force world ? !

It is a noble, expressive figure.

The description of Luria, too, admirable, or more.

The ' bared black arms held out into the sun from
the tent opening '—what a picture !—and the laugh
when the horse drops his forage—one *knows* Luria
from henceforth.

Finely characteristic, the ' You too have thought
that.'

> Bury it . . . so I write the Signory.

I think you ought to have the preposition, either
by ' Bury it . . . write I to the Signory,' or by putting
the ' to ' into the text as it is, which would not ruffle
the line too much.

> And yet renounce the same, its hour gone by.

This eloquence of Bracchio should be quite un-
involved—now should it not ?—the connection of
the two different sentences run clearly. Why not
without the inversion ?

> Have ever proved too much for Florentines
> Even for the best and bravest of ourselves—
> *If* in the struggle, when the soldier's sword
> Before the statist's hand should sink its point,
> And to the calm head, yield, the violent hand,
> Virtue on virtue still have fallen away
> Before ambition—

By shifting a few of the unimportant words so,
you make it clear to run and read. And then by
this shifting, you escape a rather questionable-

M

looking opposition of ' after ' and ' before,' in ' If virtue *after* virtue still have fallen *before* ambition.'

> So shall in him rebellion be less guilt,
> And punishment for me the easier task.

I propose, still without the inversion—

> So shall rebellion be less guilt in *him*,
> And punishment the easier task for *me*.

Is not the emphasis better marked so ?

> Even these reasons while I urge them most—

This sounds to my ear *numerically* a weak line— this setting of ' Even ' as a dissyllable to open a line. ' Why, even these reasons while I urge them most ' would seem to give more freedom—will you ring it, and later ?

> And which it took for earnest, &c.

Did you mean to write ' All which ' ?   A slip of the pen perhaps ?

> Florence, to feel, in someone over me.

I quite understand—but the construction is not clear notwithstanding. A word will do it. And how fine and joyous and generous all this is of Luria ! And this turning (afterwards) from the east's ' drear vastness,' and the acclimating of his soul to the west . . . noble it is, as he spoke it.

Yes, and how worthy note, the truly great ones.

If you put ' *that* those same great ones,' you make it clearer. To apprehend the construction at once, the reader seeks a ' that,' it seems to me. The thought is excellent.

Convinces me . . . no child's play was the past.

Now if you wrote straightforwardly ' Convinces me the past was no child's play '— is there an objection ? Because there is a ' most say ' in the next line which occupies the precisely corresponding place to ' child's play ' and, so, jingles. Or is it a mere fancy of mine ? And then, where nothing is gained by an inversion, the simpler form seems better.

Now make the duplicate, if this should fail.

Query, ' . . . *lest* this should fail ' ?

' So plays.'—

Is the connection clear ? Or the meaning even ? Do you mean ' So in plays.' . . . ' It is so in plays.' But then you set your readers thinking . . . or rather looking through the dictionary.

ACT II

> Well, Florence, shall I reach thee, pierce thy heart
> Thro' all the safeguards, pass 'twixt all the play
> Of arrowy wiles.

Does it not look, at least, like a confusion of metaphor? Though a person may be defended from a dagger, for instance, by a shower of arrows preventing the approach of an assassin, still it would simplify it, if you made the means of defence the sevenfold of a shield, or the subtle linkings of a mail. Is it worth a consideration?

> Nor man's device, nor heaven to keep in mind
> The wickedness forgot too soon.

Might it be written

> Nor man's device, nor heaven's pure memory
> Of wickedness forgot on earth too soon
> But thy own heart,—'tis Hell, I trust, and thee
> That firm thou keep, &c.

I do not understand exactly—' 'tis Hell and thee.'— If you wrote

> It is for hell and thee
> To keep thy first course firmly to the end,

that would be clear—but would it be as you desire?

> And this wild mass of rage that I prepare,
> Luria, to launch against thee.

Do observe that this line and a half seem to have
fallen down from the height of the argument into
a strange place.   It is a distracted construction . . .
a little.   Would it be straighter to be more coherent,
if you wrote it somewhat thus :

                  turn aside
  For gratitude a single step, or shame . . .
  Grace thou this Luria, . . . this wild mass of rage
  I now prepare to launch against thyself, . . .
  With other payment.

For the expected wreath the strange blow came

Query—

The strange blow came for the expected wreath.

When Florence on plain fact pronouncing so
Could to such actions such an end decree—for mort le
  mort.

Tell me if an air of stiffness is not given by such
unnecessary inversions.   You throw important words,
too, at arm's length from their emphasis by it in
this instance.   Query—

Could judge such actions worthy of such an end.
                    not one
  Possible way of getting his fair fame.

If you repeat ' one,'
                      not one
  One possible way of getting his fair fame;

you strengthen the line, do you not ?   It seems a
willowy line otherwise.

> Devoted brows are to be crowned no longer
> Whom the smile paid, or word of praise, so well.

It is not clear——will not be to the reader, I
think—and a word or two more will ensure the
desired purpose.

> And, either way the fight's event he keeps.

It would be clearer and more unquestionable if
you wrote it, perhaps,

> And, let the fight end either way, he keeps.

This is the pettiest, paltriest, criticism of straws !
But just these straws hide the path, with you, sometimes.

> Pisa's last safeguard, all to intercept
> The rage of her implacablest of foes
> From Pisa.

Does the construction seem clear to yourself ?
Give us a little light.

> Therefore should the preponderating gift
> Of love and trust Florence was first to throw,
> Made you her own not Pisa's, void the scale.

I dare to propose ' *Which* made you her own not

Pisa's, void the scale,' because without it, the thread
of meaning gets entangled.

> And after all you will look gallantly
> Found dead here with that letter in your breast.

Very fine all this. I infinitely admire the whole
interview between Luria and Tiburzio—nothing can
be nobler. And the suppressed emotion *tells*.

> That as they know my deeds, with me they deal.

Why not ' That as they know my deeds they deal
with *me* ' ?

> Oh this Luria ! how great he is.
> The palm trees and the pyramid o'er all. . .

Don't coop up such a wide desert-line by the
contracted ' o'er,' jingling with ' all ' too. There
is room for ' over all ' surely, said out broadly.

> Treachery even—that such an one say.

The line seems to want strengthening by another
syllable—' Of treachery even. . . ? ' I only ask.

ACT III

Nor did this urge me, that if judge I must.

You will wonder when I complain of darkness
here—but certainly it is doubtfully worded—' Nor
did this urge me.'

> Each knowledge that broke through a heart to life,
> Each reasoning it cost a brain to yield.

A noble first line and thought ! And should you
not interpose a word in the second ? . . . ' Each
reasoning that it cost,' &c., or if you wrote. . .
' Each reasoning which to work out, cost a brain.'
Oh, it is only that the second line appears to sound
feebly in comparison with the great thing it has to
say, and also with the great line preceding it in
utterance. And then I write down what comes
into my head. Braccio's justification of Florence
is (for the rest) very subtle and noble—one half
forgives Braccio in it.

> Who did the several acts yourselves gave names.

You mean ' Gave names to.' Then why not say
' yourselves have named ' ? For clearness.

> He goes on like the brute he is *against*
> It falls before him, or he dies in his course.

Did you mean to write ' against,' and not rather
' until ' ?   The interest is carried nobly on through
this act.   Poor Luria !

ACT IV

Just where you left them blacks and whites you'll find.

Why not, O you inverter ?—

You'll find just where you left them, blacks and whites.

I like the thought so much.

Your tricks with me too well succeed for that.

Query—Your tricks succeed with me too well
for that ?

Is there an objection ?

Duty to do O have I, and faith to keep.

Query—' Duty O have I to do.'   Puccio speaks
admirably yet like a soldier.

Set for your heart on stoutness ne'er so firm.

Which line I do not very much like.   I don't
like a firm stoutness, or a heart set firmly on stoutness . . . read it any way, and I set about objections.

Far too plain
Souls show themselves for men to choose and read.

It seems to me that the whole of this passage
is somewhat diffusely given, and not distinctly.

If this soul-reading is so easily achievable by boys, is it a *consequence* that Luria should be read wrong? Will you look and raise your wand once?

How thinkest thou? I have turned on them their arms.

Is there an objection to making this clear by repeating the word ' light '?

> I have turned their light on *them*.

Then in the next line—

> A transient thing was this our thirst of war.

If you wrote ' They called our thirst of war a transient thing,' you allow the reader to see at a glance what otherwise he will seek studiously. And so worthy of all admiration it is, this discourse of Husein's with his true doctrine, that ' all work is fighting.'

>   I proclaim
> The angel in thee and reject the sprites.

A fine expression—the first; but why not write ' spirits ' at length?

> Above them which still safelier bids them live.

Not a very favourite line perhaps of mine—but the ' *weaklier* ' must stand so near it, anywise. See below.

The word ' break ' too ends two several lines.

My belief is that the whole passage will strike you as diffused and that you will teach it to coil up gathering strength. Domizia speaks her speech for the rest eloquently and well—she has her side of truth like the rest—and one feels for poor Luria so much the more—' 'Tis well for them to see—but him ? ' Poor Luria, how great and benignant in circumstances which makes misanthropes of other men! It is very fine . . . all to the end.

ACT V

Even affects the other course to chose.

I do not like the lines which begin 'Even,' making a dissyllable of it ; they sound weak to me. But there is an objection here besides, because . . . observe the meaning . . . you do not mean to say ' it even *affects* the other course,' &c., but that ' It affects even the other *course*,' &c. Do you see ? I am always making that mistake myself, and everybody makes it . . . but there is a right and a wrong way after all. If you wrote ' affects the other course even, left to chose ' or ' Affects even the other course we have to chose '—see?—I admire the dialogue here. It is suggestive and full besides.

> And having disbelieved your innocence
> How can she trust your magnanimity ?

True and overcoming . . . and put so excellently well. The suggested pathos of this situation . . . how deep it is! Poor great Luria! I feel that I ought not to be able to count the trefoil when lifted to the summit of a mountain. But I do not like that little ending word to Puccio's speech, 'You bid.' 'Bid'—the accent on 'bid.' Won't you say 'you bid me,' at least?

Being the thrice chivalric soul we know.

Is there an objection to saying . . . 'He being the,' &c., because there seems a weakness otherwise— *to the ear*, I mean.

As greater now who better still hath been.

Why not . . . 'As greater now who hath been better still'? It is more natural, more clear, less stiff perhaps.

God's finger marks distinction all so fine, &c.

I admire this excellent true thought, which cannot be said better nor clearer.

Whose lambent play so all innocuous seemed.

Or . . . 'Whose lambent play seemed so innocuous.' Why object to natural sequence of words?

The everlasting minute of creation
Arrested.

Fine, that is. But I do not see what business 'arrested' has—it *darkens*. I fancy 'suspended' might convey the thought—might it not? But perhaps neither word is needed.

The play ends nobly, bearing itself up to its own height to the last . . . and leaving an impression which must be an emotion with all readers. Do think that just my first thoughts have been set down in these notes, and take them at their worth—or noworth.

E. B. B.

ROBERT BROWNING'S ANSWERS TO QUESTIONS CONCERNING SOME OF HIS POEMS [1]

By A. Allen Brockington

In the early days of 1888 a club, styled ' The Day's End Club,' was formed in the city of Exeter, to study contemporary literature.

On February 18, 1889, a member read to the Club six of Robert Browning's shorter poems. He had paraphrased some, and his reading and notes provoked much discussion. The Rev. Sackville A. Berkeley, who had become acquainted with Browning at Oxford, offered to write to the poet, and state the difficulties of the members.

Answering the questions Browning wrote :

' I am delighted that you remember me, and have interest enough in my writings to put the questions concerning them which you obligingly do : I suppose the readiest way of answer will be to return them with what explanations occur to me duly appended.'

[1] Reprinted from the *Cornhill Magazine*, March 1914.

This letter, dated February 22, 1889, was written at 29 De Vere Gardens. Though Browning was within a few months of his death at this time, the handwriting shows no trace of weakness. It is as firm and characteristic as in those of his earlier life.

The following is a copy of the paper. The poet's answers are italicised.

QUERIES

My Last Duchess

Was she in fact shallow and easily and equally well pleased with any favour : or did the Duke so describe her as a supercilious cover to real and well justified jealousy ?

> *As an excuse—mainly to himself—for taking revenge on one who had unwittingly wounded his absurdly pretentious vanity, by failing to recognise his superiority in even the most trifling matters.*

' " Frà Pandolf " by design ' :
By what design ?

> *To have some occasion for telling the story, and illustrating part of it.*

In a Gondola

Was *she* true, or in the conspiracy ?
  Out of it.

Earth's Immortalities

' Love ' :

Is the refrain—' (Love me for ever !) ' cynical, or sad, or trustful ?

  A mournful comment on the short duration of the conventional ' For Ever ! '

Parting at Morning

' And the need of a world of men for me ' :

Is this an expression by her of her sense of loss of him, or the despairing cry of a ruined woman ?

  Neither : it is his *confession of how fleeting is the belief (implied in the first part) that such raptures are self-sufficient and enduring—as for the time they appear.*

The question concerning ' Parting at Morning ' expresses a difficulty that has been felt by many readers. Indeed one would hardly conclude that Browning referred to the ' Sun ' in the third line :

  And straight was a path of gold for him.

In the preface to his Selections published in 1872, Browning says :

A few years ago, had such an opportunity presented itself, I might have been tempted to say a word in reply to the objections my poetry was used to encounter.   Time has kindly co-operated with my disinclination to write the poetry and the criticism besides.   The readers I am at last privileged to expect meet me fully half-way ; and if, from the fitting standpoint, they must still ' censure me in their wisdom,' they have previously ' awakened their senses that they may the better judge.'   Nor do I apprehend any more charges of being wilfully obscure, unconscientiously careless, or perversely harsh.

The passages which follow will explain the questions and answers which were given by the poet.

My Last Duchess

Ferrara

That's my last Duchess painted on the wall,
Looking as if she were alive.   I call
That piece a wonder, now : Frà Pandolf's hands
Worked busily a day, and there she stands.
Will't please you sit and look at her ?   I said

' Frà Pandolf ' by design : for never read
Strangers like you that pictured countenance,
The depth and passion of its earnest glance,
But to myself they turned (since none put by
The curtain I have drawn for you, but I)
And seemed as they would ask me, if they durst,
How such a glance came there ; so, not the first
Are you to turn and ask thus. Sir, 'twas not
Her husband's presence only, called that spot
Of joy into the Duchess' cheek : . . . .
. . . . She thanked men—good ! but thanked
Somehow—I know not how—as if she ranked
My gift of a nine-hundred-years-old name
With anybody's gift.   ·

EARTH'S IMMORTALITIES

Love

So the year's done with !
  (*Love me for ever !*)
All March begun with,
  April's endeavour ;
May-wreaths that bound me
  June needs must sever ;
Now snows fall round me,
  Quenching June's fever—
  (*Love me for ever !*).

PARTING AT MORNING

Round the cape of a sudden came the sea,
 And the sun looked over the mountain's rim :
And straight was a path of gold for him,
And the need of a world of men for me.

INDEX TO TITLES OF POEMS

INDEX TO FIRST LINES OF POEMS

PRINTED BY
SPOTTISWOODE AND CO. LTD., COLCHESTER
LONDON AND ETON